EMPLOYEE PARTICIPATION
IN EUROPE

EMPLOYEE PARTICIPATION IN EUROPE

Herman Knudsen

SAGE Publications
London • Thousand Oaks • New Delhi

First published 1995

SAGE Publications Ltd
6 Bonhill Street
London EC2A 4PU

SAGE Publications Inc
2455 Teller Road
Thousand Oaks, California 91320

SAGE Publications India Pvt Ltd
32, M-Block Market
Greater Kailash – I
New Delhi 110 048

British Library Cataloguing in Publication data

A catalogue record for this book is
available from the British Library

   ISBN 0-8039-7542-2

Library of Congress catalog card number 95-69060

Typeset by M Rules
Printed in Great Britain by Redwood Books, Trowbridge,
Wiltshire

Contents

Acknowledgements

Work on this book was undertaken between 1990 and late 1994. It proceeded through phases of intensive study and writing as well as 'quiet' phases where other obligations, mainly teaching, took all my time. I wish to thank my colleagues in the governing bodies of Aalborg University for making the intensive periods possible by granting me two research fellowships, each of half a year's duration.

The inclusion of Spain in the study would have been extremely difficult without the three months' stay I enjoyed at the University of Seville in the beautiful spring of 1991. I am very grateful to Professor Fermin Rodriguez-Sañudo and Professor Joaquin García Murcia for inviting me and guiding me through the details of Spanish industrial relations. Financially, the stay was supported by the Spanish state, Junta de Andalucia, and the Danish Social Science Research Council.

Several colleagues have been of great help by reading and suggesting improvements to draft versions of parts of the manuscript. I would especially like to mention: Professors Fermin Rodriguez-Sañudo (Sevilla), Joaquin García Murcia (Sevilla/Oviedo) and Andoni Kaiero Uria (Bilbao), for comments on the chapter on Spain; research fellow Hans-Joachim Sperling (Paderborn/Bochum), for comments on the chapter on Germany; lecturer Paul Brook (Manchester), for comments on the chapter on Britain; Professor Reinhard Lund (Aalborg), for comments on the chapter on Denmark; Professor Richard Hyman (Warwick) and lecturer Jens Lind (Aalborg), for comments on the draft manuscript.

Assistance of a more practical, but no less important, character has been given by Dorthe Andersen, Anette Bech and Karina Clausen on processing the text, by Dorte Madsen on improving my English, and by Anni Busk and Susanne Aagaard who, as librarians, helped to chase the relevant literature.

Who helped me to get my feet back on the ground when I was down? Rikke, my life companion. She also put up with my often long periods of – sometimes mental, sometimes physical – absence.

Who helped me to contain the subject of participation and be able to stick to it, despite its immense contradictions and evasiveness? One important inspiration was Leonard Cohen, the Canadian poet and viii *Employee participation in Europe*

singer, with these words in his song called *Democracy*: *"It's coming from the feel that it ain't exactly real, or it's real, but it ain't exactly there."*

Herman Knudsen
Aalborg University

List of Abbreviations

BDA	Bundesvereinigung der Deutschen Arbeitgeberverbände (the German Employers' Confederation)
CBI	Confederation of British Industry
CC.OO	Comisiones Obreras (Workers' Committees, Spain)
CDU	Christlich-Demokratische Union (the Christian Democratic Party, Germany)
CEC	Commission of the European Communities
CEEP	Confederation of European Public Enterprises
CEOE	Confederación Española de Organizaciones Empresariales (the Spanish Employers' Confederation)
CSU	Christlich-Soziale Union (the Christian Social Party, Germany)
DA	Dansk Arbejdsgiverforening (the Danish Employers' Confederation)
DGB	Deutsche Gewerkschaftsbund (the German Trade Union Confederation)
EC	European Community or European Communities
EEC	European Economic Community
EF	The European Foundation for the Improvement of Living and Working Conditions [also abbreviated to the European Foundation]
EIRR	*European Industrial Relations Review*
ET	Estatuto de los Trabajadores (Workers' Statute, Spain)
ETUC	European Trade Union Confederation
ETUI	European Trade Union Institute
EU	European Union
EWC	European Works Council
FDP	Freie Demokratische Partei (the Free Democratic Party, Germany)
IG Metall	Industriegewerkschaft Metall (the Industrial Union of Metalworkers, Germany)
ILO	International Labour Office
LO	Landsorganisationen i Danmark (the Danish Trade Union Confederation)
TUC	Trades Union Congress (Britain)

| UGT | Unión General de Trabajadores (Workers' General Union, Spain) |
| UNICE | Union of Industries of the EC |

Introduction

This book deals with relations between employers and employees within the European Union. More precisely, its focus is on the participation of employees in management decisions within the workplaces and companies of European Union countries.

Participation is a popular concept. Almost everybody seems to be in favour of it – managers, trade unionists and politicians alike. Nevertheless, employee participation has proved to be a highly controversial issue in the relations between trade unions and employers' organizations and between nation states within the European Union. Since 1970 the Commission of the EC/EU has put forward several proposals for a common regulation of employee participation; yet it has proved extremely difficult to have the more comprehensive initiatives adopted by the Council of Ministers.

The Commission of the EC has often expressed the notion of a specific 'European social model', partly as an already existing reality, and partly as a desirable goal for European integration in the field of social and industrial relations. No doubt both Catholic and social democratic social ideas have influenced the formation of this concept. Its central tenet is that harmonious social relations can only be established and maintained if society takes the interests of workers and other dependent groups into consideration, and accommodates them by constructing institutions of a socially integrative character. This idea again rests on the European experience that a non-integrated labour movement can indeed have disrupting consequences for the existing social order, as was the case in the revolutions following the First World War, the Spanish Civil War, and the widespread strike movements of 1968 and the years after. It also rests on the positive experience that industrial relations systems based on a clear recognition of the aspirations of the labour movement and on social compromises between potentially antagonistic class interests have proved to be quite successful, socially as well as economically, as witness German society since the Second World War.

The institutionalization of the participation of employees in management decisions has been seen as one important pillar of a European social model. In fact, to a large extent it is already there, given the fact that the great majority of EU member countries have established specific institutions with the aim of safeguarding employee participation, and given the long tradition of such institutions in many of these countries.

Why, then, have the protracted attempts of the Commission to 'Europeanize' this pillar, to provide a common framework for employee participation, encountered such great difficulties in being accepted by the member states? This question has been the point of departure for my study and has also given rise to a whole series of related questions, necessary for gaining an understanding of the dynamics of employee participation as well as European social integration within this particular area.

1   *Why participation?*   What were the underlying motives behind the introduction of participatory institutions? What have been the positions of the industrial relations' actors, notably trade unions, employers' organizations and governments, in relation to the development of participation? Has participation evolved in a linear way, or has it rather been connected with cyclical movements within the economic, political and ideological spheres? Has it been favoured by structural change such as the spread of new technologies and the internationalization of the economy?
2   *How participation?*   Through which different forms may employee participation be practised, and how are these forms related to specific national traditions and the total industrial relations system in which they are situated? What are the positions of the social actors in relation to different forms of participation? How intense is the participation: does it amount to a real sharing of decision-making powers over important issues at workplace and company level?
3   *An EU participation model?*   What are the prospects for a more uniform pattern of workforce participation across the EU member states? Are there trends towards a convergence between the different national systems of participation: a convergence either based on a normative harmonization within the EU or on more 'organic' unifying forces such as technological change and economic internationalization? Or is greater diversity a more likely prospect? And, finally, is the notion of a European social model a realistic possibility, or is it mainly an ideological concept exploited by European integrationists?

These questions have provided the main guidelines for the research underlying this book. The purpose of the study has been twofold: to reach a thorough understanding of employee participation in its national settings by analysing it from historical, sociological as well as comparative angles, and to relate these analyses to the theme of European integration within the industrial relations area. I have wanted to examine employee participation at the juncture between national pasts and a present which is increasingly characterized by European integration and internationalization.

In my research I have concentrated on the participation systems of four EU member states, namely Germany, Britain, Spain and Denmark, and on the relevant initiatives taken at the European Community level. The selection of the four countries was based on the consideration that they represent markedly different industrial relations and participation systems, and therefore very well illustrate the diversity among EU member states. Among them, Britain and Germany can be said to represent the two opposite poles of the EU debate, while Spain represents the southern European and Denmark the Scandinavian tradition. Of course, these four countries do not cover in any representative way the whole range of national diversities within the EU. However, rather than attempting to include all the national participation systems within the EU my ambition has been to analyse a few of them in some depth, to trace their origins and development so that national diversities, concerning institutions as well as policies, become explicable. As for the 'neglected' member states, I must refer to the short description of the institutional arrangements of all the EU countries given in chapter 1 of this book, and to Kolvenbach & Hanau (1987/94) who give very detailed descriptions of national participation institutions in Europe.

The structure of the book is as follows. In chapter 1, I address the questions of 'why' and 'how' participation occurs at a general level. Drawing on earlier research, I discuss the concept of employee participation and its different dimensions, establish distinctions between different types and intensities of participation, and between democratic, integrative and productive rationales behind the introduction of participation. Further, employee participation is presented as a mode of regulation which forms part of a workplace regime together with other elements, such as unilateral employer decision-making and collective bargaining. Finally, the question is raised whether there is a tendency for national participation systems to converge into a uniform, European pattern.

Chapters 2–5 consist of profiles of the national participation systems of Germany, Britain, Spain and Denmark. For each country I locate the participation system within the wider industrial relations system, and analyse its origins, development, forms and intensity. Special sections deal with the impact of new technology and the positions of the industrial relations parties. In each chapter I conclude by summing up the characteristic features of the national participation system in question.

In chapter 6, I put the national profiles together, compare the

development and characteristics of the four national systems, and evaluate the strength of a common European legacy *vis-à-vis* the national
traditions and trajectories. The results suggest strong sources for continued diversity between countries, and the country portraits thus
hardly add up to a European family picture.

Chapter 7 is played out in Brussels. Here I present the various initiatives taken in the field by the European Commission since the early
1970s, relate them to the existing regulations in the member states, and
attempt to explain why the more far-reaching initiatives have had great
difficulties in being adopted. I also analyse the possibilities opened up
by the Maastricht Treaty and the repercussions, for a possible
European model, of the new decision-making procedures as well the
adoption of the European Works Council directive in September 1994.

Chapter 8 looks at the impact of information technology on
employee participation. I reject the contention that new technologies
constitute some sort of compelling reason for a general growth and
convergence of participation. It is also demonstrated that there are
wide variations across EU member states as far as participation in the
planning and introduction of new technology is concerned, and that
the type and intensity of participation wanted by employers differ substantially from the aspirations of the trade union movement.

In the conclusion I pull together the main results, and look at the
future prospects for employee participation in a European context.
Rather than a practical reality, the European model is still best
described as a vague shadow of national models. Yet, the contours of
the shadow have changed. In the 1970s, German institutional arrangements provided the model for the proposals debated within the
European Community, and a total harmonization on this basis was
envisaged. In the 1990s, the goals are more modest. The attempt is to
find flexible solutions able to secure a common minimum level of participation, but also allowing for the diversity of national traditions and
institutions.

1

Employee Participation: Concept and Context

Participation is an extremely plastic concept: it can be moulded into many different forms, and acquires a wide variety of meanings for different groups of social actors. This is true in general, and also within the area of this study: the participation of employees in management decisions at workplace and company level.

In this chapter I shall attempt to define and delineate some central practical and theoretical characteristics of employee participation as well as the context within which it is situated, by addressing especially the questions of *how* and *why* participation is taking place. I will start by presenting some taxonomies of the rich variations of existing forms of employee participation, then move on to the more theoretical questions about the *raison d'être* of participation and its *locus* within workplace industrial relations.

Types of participation and participatory institutions

Institutions for participation at workplace and company level may formally originate from three different *sources*: they can be based on statutory regulation, collective bargaining or decisions taken unilaterally by the employer. The same type of institution may rest on different sources in different countries. This is, for example, the case for the French *comité d'entreprise* (based on legislation), the Danish *samarbejdsudvalg* (based on a national collective agreement) and the British joint consultation committee (usually based on a unilateral employer decision). These bodies have in common that they consist of both employer and employee representatives and aim to be a forum for discussion of certain managerial decisions.

Another important distinction is between *direct* and *indirect* participation, or between *individual* and *representative* participation (de la Villa 1980; Gold & Hall 1990). Direct participation means that the individual employee takes over or is drawn into certain managerial decisions which have traditionally been taken by management alone. This may take several forms: the delegation of a greater degree of discretion over the immediate work tasks, the creation of autonomous groups or quality circles, meetings at workgroup, workshop or department level. The direct form of participation is in general only applied to lower-level management decisions, typically decisions regarding how work operations shall be carried out, although there are also examples of direct employee involvement in middle or higher-level management decisions concerning technical and organizational change, notably through project groups.

Indirect participation implies that the participation of employees takes place through representatives; for instance, shop stewards or works council members. Contrary to the direct form, it is based on the articulation of collective interests. Typical institutions for indirect participation are (a) shop-steward meetings with management, the shop stewards being elected by and representing the members of a specific trade union at the workplace; (b) works councils, i.e. bodies elected by all employees at the workplace with a right to meet regularly with the management; and (c) joint committees which are mixed bodies consisting of management as well as employee representatives. In companies with several workplaces and in groups of companies, the participation bodies established at workplace level may be supplemented by central bodies for the whole company or the whole group. A further possibility is (d) the representation of employees on the company board or a supervisory board alongside shareholder representatives. Thus, indirect participation may take place both within the operational units (workplace or plant level) and the financial units (company or firm level).

If the dichotomy of direct and indirect participation is combined with the above-mentioned three different sources, we get the six different types of participation shown in table 1.1. All of these six types of participation exist in the real world, although in varying degrees of importance as the following examples will demonstrate.

Type 1   While several countries have had state-supported programmes to further the direct involvement of workers – as for instance the German 'humanization of working life' programme (Jakobsen & Clausen 1991) – legal regulations on direct employee participation are rare. One exception is the French legislation of 1982 on 'expression groups' which obliges establishments with 50 employees or more to organize meetings at regular intervals where the employees can directly

Table 1.1   *Types of employee participation*

Source	Form	
	Direct	Indirect
Law	1	4
Collective agreement	2	5
Employer decision	3	6

express their opinions on 'the content and organization of their work, and on the structuring and implementation of measures to improve working conditions in their company' (Gold & Hall 1990: 32–5). It should also be mentioned that in several countries there are statutory provisions entitling all employees to receive information on certain company issues.

Type 2 Direct participation based on collective agreements is also a relatively rare phenomenon, especially at a national or sectoral level. The 'cooperation experiments' in Denmark from 1969 to 1972 followed an agreement between the employers' confederation and the main trade union organization. Among other things, it included the creation of project groups and semi-autonomous groups in some enterprises for a certain period (Christensen 1979: 71–9). Somewhat more frequently, direct participation is regulated by collective agreements at company level. One example is from Germany where the Volkswagen management introduced quality circles from the beginning of the 1980s. In 1986, the trade union IG Metall managed to negotiate an agreement with the management, granting the works council the right to take part in decisions concerning the operations of the quality circles (Gold & Hall 1990: 31).

Type 3 Unilateral employer decisions constitute the most common foundation for direct participation, but it is rather complicated to assess the extent and trends regarding this type of participation. Recent studies indicate a growth in specific forms of direct participation such as quality circles and team briefings (Regini 1992). Two studies from the 1970s demonstrated that British and German shopfloor managers respectively allowed workers considerably more discretion in their work than did their French colleagues (Gallie 1978; Maurice et al. 1986). On the European level, however, there are no reliable comparable data available covering all forms of direct participation. Neither will they be easy to collect, partly because many direct participation practices have an essentially informal character, and partly because different terms are used for the same phenomena both across and within the different countries. Notwithstanding these difficulties, there is hope for improved knowledge in this area. In 1993 a study aiming to compare the incidence and forms of direct participation across the European Community member states was initiated by the European Foundation in Dublin.

Type 4 Indirect participation based on legislation is relatively widespread in Europe. It is in particular participation of this type that the European Community has attempted to generalize through regulation based on directives. Among the 12 EU member states, eight – Belgium, Germany, France, Greece, Luxembourg, the Netherlands, Portugal and Spain – have statutory provisions for the establishment of works councils or joint committees which to varying degrees are empowered to take part in workplace decisions (Gold & Hall 1990: 7). Five countries – Denmark, Germany, France, Luxembourg and the Netherlands – have legal provisions for employee representation on company boards, while in Ireland, Greece and Portugal similar provisions apply only to state-owned enterprises (Gold & Hall 1990: 15–20). It should also be mentioned that there are provisions for participation in relation to certain specific issues in all the member states, on the basis of EU directives. As an example, the EC 'framework directive' on health and safety of 1989 obliged those member states which had not already done so to introduce legislation on the participation of employee representatives in decisions concerning health and safety (Gill 1993).

Type 5   Indirect participation based on collective agreement is especially important in countries such as Britain and Ireland where legislation on participation is of less significance. The participation may take place through shop stewards or special bodies designed with a view to furthering participation. In Denmark cooperation committees operate according to national agreements reached between the leading organizations of employers and trade unions in both the private and public sectors. In Italy *rappresentanze sindicali aziendali* are bodies with certain similarities to works councils. Their frames of reference are defined by labour legislation, but they are constituted by the trade unions, and their precise participation rights are determined through collective bargaining (Biagi 1990). In a number of countries, collective agreements, often at local level, provide for the setting up of specialized joint committees where employee representatives participate in decisions in areas such as health and safety and training.

Type 6   Finally, employers may choose on their own initiative to establish some form of indirect participation, for instance by allowing the employees one or more seats on the company board, or by setting up a joint consultative committee with representation from management and employees. Both forms can be found, although not extensively, in Britain where there are no legal provisions for employee participation, except on health and safety matters.

Intensity of participation and employee influence

Gold & Hall propose two definitions of the intensity of participation: a brief one where 'intensity equates with the degree of employee influence afforded by participatory arrangements at a given level' (1990: 4), and a much more complex definition where the following variables have to be taken into account: (a) the range of subjects covered; (b) the stage at which participation takes place; (c) the methods used (information disclosure, consultation and co-determination); (d) the combination of diverse levels (the number of levels where participation is established from workshop to company level); and (e) the degree to which the provisions on participation are actually implemented (1990: 25).

In my view, the first of these definitions is too abstract and the second too comprehensive to provide an adequate understanding of the intensity and influence aspect of participation. Instead, I propose that participation intensity can be defined as the combined result of two dimensions. One is the degree of influence which is assigned to employees and/or their representatives (stretching from the receiving of information, over consultation and co-determination or co-decision, to cases of unilateral employee decision-making). The other is the range and importance of subjects covered by participatory decisions (stretching from the colour of the toilet paper to important decisions such as production strategies, mergers and closures). In brief, the intensity of participation is the strength of employee decision-making powers multiplied by the number and importance of issues covered by participatory decision-making.

This is still not a very clear definition, so it will be necessary to have a closer look at the two dimensions which enter into it. The first dimension concerns the degree of influence afforded to employees. Here, a common distinction is between three distinct levels, namely disclosure of information, consultation, and co-decision or co-determination (Rodriguez-Sañudo 1979; Gold & Hall 1990). Provisions obliging the employer to disclose and forward *information* on certain issues, e.g. the financial or employment situation of the firm, constitute the weakest form of influence. In itself the information does not equip the employees with any influence over the issues in question, but indirectly it can be useful as a necessary basis for gaining influence. If employees do not know the plans of management they are also unable to influence them.

Provisions demanding that the employer must hear the opinions of the employee representatives, or *consult* with them, before making changes related to working or employment conditions, are somewhat more powerful. Formally seen, it is true that a right to be consulted still bestows no influence, but it does give employee representatives an opportunity to come forward with criticisms as well as alternative ideas concerning how to handle the issue in question. Furthermore, consultations may develop into negotiations and result in informal or formal agreements between the two parties. Whether this will happen or not depends on the industrial relations climate of the workplace as well as the exact wording of the provisions for consultation, for instance whether the employer is only obliged to receive the opinions of the employee side or also obliged to discuss these opinions. An example of a strong form of consultation can be found in the Danish cooperation agreements. These oblige the employer to show good will and to attempt to reach agreement with the employee representatives on a number of issues.

The strongest form of participatory decision-making exists when the decision has to be taken jointly by the employer and the employee side. Joint regulation may be expressed through *co-decision*, i.e. a situation where a decision can only be taken if the two parties agree, a third party being entitled to arbitrate if they fail to do so, or through *co-determination* where the decision-making body is constituted on the basis of the parity principle (50–50 representation), and where again a third party has the final word in case of disagreement between the two sides (Martín Valverde et al. 1991: 253–4). Both co-decision and co-determination play an important part in German industrial relations, but joint regulation is also applied within certain areas in some of the other EU countries (Gold & Hall 1990).

An even stronger form of participation may be said to exist when the employees themselves are enabled to make decisions, as in the French concept of *autogestion* and the British *workers' control* (Poole 1986a: 82–123; Lucas Marín 1990). These concepts, however, are on the borderline of a discourse on participation because they express a challenge to the whole authority structure of capitalist enterprises, and therefore are more meaningfully interpreted as forms of resistance to, and conflict within, this structure. In my view, unilateral decision-making by one party lies outside the scope of participation, as participation presupposes an interplay between two parties.

Yet, in relation to direct participation, a concept of unilateral employee decision-making is indispensable. Direct participation may be based on information, consultation and joint regulation, but to a large extent it is practised by transferring low-level management decisions to the employees themselves, be it in individual jobs or through autonomous groups. An important point is, however, that such transfers of decision-making powers at the lowest level do not increase employee influence over strategic and tactical decisions at company or workplace level. This brings us to the next dimension relevant to the intensity of participation: the range and importance of subjects covered by participatory decision-making.

Numerous management issues may be singled out as subjects for employee participation. This will be evident especially in chapters 2 and 4 where the German and Spanish provisions on participation are presented. A traditional way of classifying types of subjects is the distinction between 'social', personnel and financial matters, where social is understood in very broad terms as not just welfare issues, but all matters related to the work and employment situation (Weiss 1987). The philosophy behind this distinction is that the main interest of the owners lies in the financial issues, where employee participation should accordingly be weak, whereas the central interest of the employees is in the 'social' area – for which reason participation here should be strong. This contention, however, is problematic. It is true that it is the work situation which immediately affects the employees in their daily life, but that does not mean that they are not interested in the financial state of the firm; this, after all, determines whether the company will survive or go under, reduce or increase its workforce and so on. Moreover, a distinction between social, personnel and financial matters appears to be inadequate for grasping the principal differences between types of decisions within firms. Inspired by organization literature, and in particular Rivero Lamas & García Blasco (1987), I will instead propose a distinction between four different types of management decisions:

1 *Strategic decisions*: the overall decisions determining the company's goals, its structure and main types of activities, major product-related investment decisions, mergers, take-overs, and partial or complete closures.
2 *Tactical decisions*: the overall decisions defining the means to realize the goals of the company, central decisions – at company or workplace level – concerning technology and work organization, principles guiding job design, personnel management, operation hours, payment systems, health and safety, etc.
3 *Operational decisions*: the more specific decisions taken, usually at department or workshop level, as to how work shall be carried out within the given technical–organizational framework: the concrete deployment of labour defined through such measures as the definition of tasks, the assigning of workers to the specified tasks, the application of payment systems, the monitoring of the labour process, the definition of shift-work schedules and the allocation of working hours for individual employees, the fixation of holiday periods, the application of health and safety prescriptions, etc.
4 *Welfare decisions*: decisions concerning company-specific welfare arrangements, such as canteen facilities, housing facilities, sports and other recreational activities, scholarships, and other forms of financial support separate from the ordinary remuneration.

The above list also represents a ranking of the importance of subjects within a company. For employers as well as for employees, strategic and tactical decisions deal with the most important subjects, whereas operational and welfare decisions concern the least important. This contention is based on an assessment of the likely consequences of the different types of decision. It is true that decisions at the operational level may have serious consequences for individual employees, but for the employees as a collective there is no doubt that the strategic and tactical decisions have the most far-reaching implications. They define the fundamental aspects of employment and working conditions.

By combining the two intensity dimensions – the strength of employee decision-making powers and the importance of subjects covered by participatory decision-making – it is now possible to visualize the typical dispersion of participation intensity in relation to management decisions. This is shown in figure 1.1 which draws on general empirical evidence within the field, and also anticipates data presented in more detail in later chapters.

Figure 1.1 reveals a pattern where participation is less intense, the more important the decisions are. It also demonstrates the diverse strengths and weaknesses of direct and indirect participation respectively. For employees, direct participation is roughly speaking only relevant in relation to decisions at the operational level; it usually affords no influence over welfare, tactical or strategic issues. Indirect participation, on the other hand, contains potentials for influence on a much wider range of decisions, although its intensity is clearly lower for decisions of a strategic or tactical nature than for those related to operational and welfare questions.

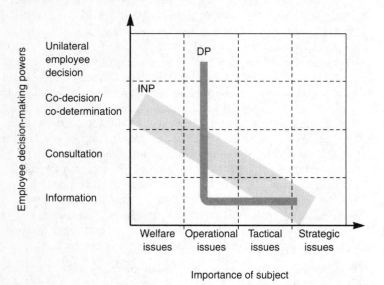

INP Area of indirect participation
DP   Area of direct participation

Figure 1.1 *Intensity of participation as a function of strength of employee decision-making powers and importance of subject*

Figure 1.1 may be read as an illustration of the degree of influence employees are able to obtain on different types of management decisions on the basis of participatory institutions typical of Western European societies today. It is important to add, however, that participation is not the only channel of influence for employees: collective action, including various forms of overt or covert resistance to and contraventions of management decisions, and collective bargaining, are other possible roads. Moreover, it is not at all unthinkable that influence gained through participation may actually reduce the possibilities of winning influence through other channels. If, for instance, employee representatives have been consulted and have given their consent to rationalization measures, they may also have formally or psychologically accepted restrictions on their freedom to fight possible negative consequences of these measures which appear at a later stage. Such possible dilemmas for workforce representatives will be presented below where participation is discussed as one of several modes of regulation at the workplace. But first we must look at the time element, as well as the various rationales behind participation.

Timing: reactive and proactive participation

Especially for decisions of a strategic or tactical nature, the time factor is often significant for the influence employees may obtain through participation. Changes in the company and workplace do not just happen overnight. Usually, they come about through a long chain of decisions ranging from problem formulation, goal-setting and choices among various technical and organizational options, to the actual introduction and practical implementation of the changes (Beirne & Ramsay 1992a). Accordingly, trade unions often demand that information must be given and consultations take place at a time sufficiently early for employee representatives to intervene in the important stages of the decision-making process.

A study on participation in relation to the introduction of new technology conducted by the European Foundation for the Improvement of Living and Working Conditions found that in all EC member states participation took place considerably more frequent in the implementation phase than in the planning phase (Fröhlich et al. 1991). In part this is a reflection of the already mentioned tendency for participatory influence to be greater in relation to operational than to tactical and strategic decisions. But it is also a reflection of the hierarchical division of labour within enterprises where ordinary employees are considered to be lacking both the competence and the legitimacy to take part in the formulation of policy, the overall goal-setting, and the choices between technological options. In particular, the Taylorist tradition has emphasized the importance of a clear division between the planning and execution of work operations, and the notion of management as an exclusive task for professional experts (Walker 1954; Braverman 1974; Wood 1989). The problem with this ideology is not that it stresses managerial skills of a professional nature, but the fact that it dismisses the relevance of employee representatives acquiring such skills.

Greater participation in the early phases of the chain of decisions would imply that participation became more *proactive*, as against the current situation where it is mainly *reactive*: it is mainly applied to the consequences of changes already decided by management rather than to those decisions and choices that determine the character of change.

A more proactive type of participation, however, poses new problems for employee representatives (Cressey 1992). In order to enter into processes of change at the stages where these are planned, and important choices made, representatives need knowledge and insight of a type they usually do not possess. The question of expertise, both individually, and as an asset accumulated by trade unions and related research institutions, becomes urgent. Proactivity to a certain extent also requires employee representatives to be willing to take on a role as co-managers, including a closer identification with company goals. The reactive versus proactive dimension will be taken up more specifically as part of the analyses of national participation institutions in the subsequent chapters.

Rationales, interests and actors behind participation

From the literature it is possible to identify different social functions performed by participation (for a comprehensive list see Bolle de Bal 1989). The different functions are connected to different rationales. Below I distinguish between three main rationales, namely democracy, social integration and economic–technical efficiency. These rationales are again connected to different social interests and actors.

Poole (1978, 1986a, b) sees workers' participation as an expression of *industrial democracy*, i.e. as a way through which employees are able to exert some influence on the conditions under which they work. As already noted, it is true that participation may imply influence, but it is certainly not always the case. To take part in a decision-making process, for example by being consulted before a final decision is taken by the management, is not the same as actually influencing the decision. Depending on the circumstances, manipulation may be a more apt description of what is going on than democracy (Dale 1954). Another reason for being suspicious of equating employee participation with industrial democracy is that there are several historical examples of participation being initiated by employers and governments who by no means wanted democratic principles to govern the workplace.

Such initiatives (which will be described in more detail later in this book) have essentially aimed to introduce participation in order to achieve *social integration* – at the workplace as well as at the societal level. Thus an American observer has commented on the far-reaching German participation system in this way (Kolvenbach & Hanau 1987/94, Gen. Sec.: 25): 'Co-determination is not intended to end the company's ability to give orders to employees, but to assure that the company's authority receives democratic legitimation through the consent of the employee.' Here a clear distinction is drawn between democracy and democratic legitimation, i.e. integration.

For employers, participation may not only give promises of a better integration of the workforce, but also of *higher efficiency*, or, as expressed by Vroom & Jago (1988: 17) 'the effective management of people and the all-important question of productivity'. Since the 1930s it has been well known among social scientists and managers that work satisfaction as well as productivity can be improved if workers are allowed to participate in decisions as to how work shall be carried out (Haire 1954; Blumberg 1968).

So, what are we talking about? Democracy, social integration or efficiency? We are talking of participation as potentially fulfilling all these three – often conflicting – social objectives. We are talking about a phenomenon borne by widely different rationales. Furthermore, these rationales are connected to different social interests and actors, each of which is seeking to achieve its own distinctive objectives.

Roughly speaking, the democratic rationale has been carried forward by the labour movement. An important goal for the labour movement has been the extension of employees' collective influence over their worklife and over the economic sphere in general. In so far as participation has been judged as furthering this objective, it has been supported by trade unions and political parties connected to the labour movement. The social integration rationale has been pursued primarily by governments, notably during wars and other periods of social upheaval where labour conflict has been perceived as a threat to the social order and the efficiency of the national economy. While governments in general are striving for social integration they are not always in favour of participation of a democratic nature; they may attempt to achieve integration through other means, as, for example, the fascist mixture of repression of the labour movement and the worshipping of an ideology of social harmony (Crouch 1993: 47–9). Finally, the efficiency rationale has mainly been supported by employers and their organizations. But, again, there is no automatic support for participation. In general, employers are only interested in participation for pragmatic reasons, i.e. if they believe it can produce better results than alternative management methods. And in general they are very critical of those forms of participation that place limitations on their right to manage (Vroom & Jago 1988).

Table 1.2 provides an overview of the different social actors and why they may be interested in participation. Again the 'may be' must be stressed, for participation is not the only road; the actors may choose to pursue their objectives and interests through alternative means.

The immediate impression gained from table 1.2 is that participation must be a battlefield rather than a field for cooperation. The potential for conflict over participation is obvious in as much as the various actors have different rationales/interests/objectives with regard to industrial relations. In order to find out why participation institutions nevertheless may be supported, or at least accepted, by all three parties, we must make things even more complicated and look at the constellations of interest more generally at societal and workplace level.

Taking the societal level first, figure 1.2 attempts to illustrate the limited possibilities for solutions based on compromises between the divergent interests of the state and the two parties of the labour market. The seven different fields of figure 1.2 represent different types of initiatives towards participation and the fate they have received. The point of the following collection of examples is that viable forms of participation can only be established if some kind of compromise or consensus has been reached between the industrial relations parties. First, the abortive initiatives:

Field 1   The British Bullock proposal of 1977, opting for a parity representation of employee representatives on company boards, was resisted by employers' organizations and by large sections of the trade union movement. It failed to be enacted.

Table 1.2   *Actors and their interests in relation to participation*

	Rationale (primary interest)	Related interests
Employees and trade unions	Influence	Gains from influence, e.g. work satisfaction, better working conditions or remuneration.
Employers and their organizations	Higher efficiency	Absence of conflict, employee motivation and commitment to company goals.
State	Social integration	Absence of social conflict, economic efficiency.

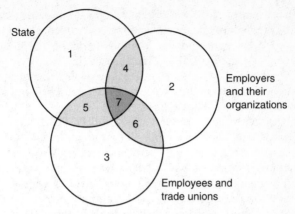

Figure 1.2   *Divergent and possible convergent interests among industrial relations actors*

Field 2   Employer-initiated consultation committees are often ignored by employees, and sometimes fought by trade unions, because they are seen as ineffective or even counterproductive instruments for furthering employee influence.

Field 3   Spanish trade union demands for representation on company boards have been opposed by employers and have not been supported by the legislative body.

Then initiatives which met with only partial success:

Field 4   Productivity committees in Britain during the Second World War aimed to improve cooperation and productivity, but were met with scepticism by large sections of the workforce.

Field 5   The change in Danish company law in 1973, granting employees representation rights on company boards, was initially met with resistance by some employers and sometimes circumvented in practice by shareholder-elected board members holding separate meetings.

And finally the successes:

Field 6   Danish cooperation committees established from 1947 on the basis of a national collective agreement.

Field 7   German works councils which today are supported by all industrial relations parties and are generally regarded as institutions promoting social integration, productive efficiency and employee influence.

It is important to stress that a specific participation arrangement can move from one field to another over time. Employee representation on

Danish company boards was originally a trade union demand opposed by both employer organizations and the government (Field 3). When a left-wing government and a unanimous parliament legislated on the issue it moved to Field 5, as described in the example above, or to Field 7 in the majority of cases where employers willingly accepted the legislation. Today it should clearly be placed in Field 7 as it is generally accepted by all the parties concerned.

Similarly with the German works councils. The first of these were established by individual employers in the nineteenth century, but were opposed by the trade union movement (Field 2). After the First World War, state legislation on works councils found only very limited support among employers and trade unions (Field 1). Only with renewed legislation after the Second World War, and especially after the pro-labour changes of legislation which took place in the 1970s, has a configuration developed where both employer organizations and trade unions positively accept and utilize the institution (Field 7).

So, although figure 1.2 visualizes two fields out of seven as fields of common interest between employers and employees, the discovery of these fields is not a simple question of finding an objectively existing common ground for participation. The common ground is only to be discovered after experiments and historical struggles between organized interests. The common ground for participation has emerged historically through social compromises which have crystallized from social struggles. Over time, the compromises have developed into lasting and relatively stable institutions because they have proved to be at least acceptable, at most advantageous, to all the industrial relations parties. This theme will be illuminated further in chapters 2–6.

From the societal level let us now move to the workplace level. How is it possible to establish viable participation structures in the individual workplace? I will address this question by introducing some considerations from game theory into the world of the workplace, my fundamental proposition being that participation will only succeed if the employer as well as the employee gains something from exercising it.

The relationship between employer and employee is marked by the independence of each of the parties but also by the mutual dependency between them. In the market sphere, the employer is independent in the sense that capital can be used alternatively; capital invested in employees can be shifted to other employees, or to machines or government bonds for that matter. Within certain limits regulated by legislation and collective agreements, the employer has the right to shut down a workplace and to dismiss the employees. The employees, for their part, are free to choose between self-employment and whatever vacant jobs there are, and free to terminate an existing employment relationship and to seek work in other establishments. This freedom, of course, is only real if alternative employment or subsistence possibilities are at hand. Often this is not the case, at least not to the extent that a given level of income can be maintained (Knudsen 1983). Here we have one of several reasons why the power relations between employers and employees must be understood as basically unequal or asymmetrical (Hyman 1975).

The degree of independence, and the relative power positions of the two parties, are underlying factors of utmost importance when the employment contract between the two parties is being fixed. However, once fixed the employment contract implies that the independence of the parties is temporarily greatly reduced. The contract obliges the employer to employ the employee, and it obliges the employee to work for the employer. The relationship is still asymmetrical, with the direction of work at one pole and the execution of work at the other, but it is now also marked by a significant degree of mutual dependency. The employer is dependent on the employees for the successful operation of the establishment, in the last instance its survival. Conversely, the employees depend upon the employer for their employment and income.

This mutual dependency is strengthened by the fact that a termination of the contract by one party will usually incur costs on the other party: employees who are dismissed usually experience a loss of income, and an employer whose employees have quit the job will have expenses hiring and training new employees. In general, these transaction costs are higher for the employer where company-based skills and experience play a central role for work performance, and lower where the skills needed are lower or of a more general character. For employees, the costs vary with the possibilities of getting an alternative job of the same quality and wage level.

Within this world of mutual dependency the two sides have both opposing and common interests. They have opposing interests in relation to how the cake, the production result, shall be divided between them, and potentially also as to how the cake shall be baked. They have common interests, however, fundamentally with respect to the survival of the workplace, but potentially also as to how it may prosper and thereby make possible both higher profits to its owners and better wages and working conditions, as well as more employment, to the employees.

The frontier between opposing and common interests is not an objective one. If the accumulation strategy of the employer is to squeeze a maximum of labour out of the employees for a minimum of remuneration, there will hardly be much room for common interests. The same will be the case if the employees share convictions of a militant or revolutionary nature, so that the employment relation is seen in purely instrumental terms, or as a lever for fighting capitalism. While there will always be an element of opposing interests between employer and employees, the definition of a space for common interests is largely a subjective matter; it requires that each party recognize the aspirations of the other, and this again will to a large extent depend on the ideology and previous experience of the parties (Nichols & Armstrong 1976). More precisely, we can say that the scope for common interests is increased *if* the mutual dependency is experienced as great, *if* both parties ideologically view a common interest perspective as possible and desirable, and *if* they furthermore have positive experiences from prior processes of cooperation.

The distinction between opposing and common interests is closely related to the difference between zero-sum and plus-sum games. Industrial conflict and collective bargaining take place essentially within a zero-sum logic (with conflict even sometimes developing into a minus-sum game). The parties act on the presumption that there is a definite sum to be divided, so that what the one party gains, the other party loses. This logic is completely understandable within capitalist work relations where competition and the pursuit of profits, if unchallenged, constantly threatens the working conditions and standard of living of working people. Only by organizing into strong workplace collectives and trade unions can employees expect to get an acceptable share of the cake (Crouch 1993).

On the other hand, the zero-sum logic corresponds to a static situation, and it does not take into consideration whether a certain way of dividing the spoils impedes or promotes the growth of the total production result. But capitalism and capitalist firms are not static. They constantly attempt to grow in order not to lose out in the competitive struggle. The creation of new plus-sums is an inherent feature of companies. Therefore there is also a scope for a plus-sum logic to be applied in industrial relations. Moreover, this scope is widened the more change and uncertainty become predominant features in the activities of companies (Fröhlich et al. 1991). Rapidly changing technologies, products and markets render cooperation an increasingly important condition for the survival of companies as well as jobs. This is where participation fits in. Cooperative and participatory decision-making processes enable the creation of new plus-sums to take place more efficiently and the gains to be divided in a less conflictual way, compared to the more 'classical' constellation where the employer is the sole agent of change, and where the employees only enter the scene *a posteriori*, negotiating over the distribution of the possible negative or positive consequences of the change. For participatory institutions to become rooted as a mode of workplace regulation, then, it is necessary that the parties concerned share the conviction that there are gains to be won by using these specific institutions instead of, say, unilateral management decisions or collective bargaining.

Before continuing and elaborating this argument, it may be appropriate to sum up where the search for a common ground for participation has led us. After departing from the observation that the different social actors are guided by different rationales and interests in relation to participation, and that participation correspondingly has different social functions, it was shown that a joint interest in participation is not easily obtained. At the societal level there is no automatic consensus between the state and the organizations of employers and employees respectively as to the desirability of employee participation. On the contrary, it is only through historical struggles, experiments and compromises that viable institutions for participation have emerged. Neither is there an automatic drive towards participation in the direct relations between employers and employees. I have argued that in order to find a common ground for participation it is necessary that the parties conceive their interests as partly common, and view their exchange relations as dealing not only with a zero-sum but also a plus-sum. Moreover, in order to become an essential part of industrial relations, participation must operate on such a common ground accepted by all parties.

Participatory institutions may exist without fulfilling these conditions; in those cases, however, they serve primarily as appendages to other institutions. For employees, participation may then be an instrument whereby employee representatives obtain a clearer picture of the strengths and weaknesses of their counterpart, a knowledge which can be used both in collective negotiations and in conflicts. For employers, participation may be a management technique useful for preventing conflicts and achieving employee consent to management decisions. Either way, participation will tend to lose its *raison d'être*.

Participation as a mode of workplace regulation

As already touched upon, participation may acquire the status of a mode of regulation. To understand the context of this significant aspect of participation it can be useful to take, as the point of departure, the fact that the enterprise or the workplace is *not* a democratically ruled organization (Pignon & Querzola 1976). The workplace is not ruled by the people, neither in the sense that everybody belonging to the organization has an equal vote when leaders are to be selected (representative democracy), nor in the sense that everybody has a say when decisions are to be taken (direct democracy). Instead, the government of the enterprise is a function of property. The owners either rule directly which is often the case in small firms, or they delegate part of their power to a manager or a group of managers who then rule the organization. The management of a firm is both a technical function concerned with financial, technical and organizational issues, and a structure of authority directing the work of the employees, the subordinates of the firm (Hill 1981: 16).

The structure of authority is reflected in the employment contract – be it individual or collective, tacit or written – which fundamentally expresses the fact that the employee sells his/her labour power (and the right to decide over it) to the employer who in exchange undertakes to pay out a certain remuneration. The right to manage, including the right to direct labour, is thus basically a prerogative of the employer, and is based on the power derived from property. It is interesting to note that the nature of the employment relationship was used by early bourgeois philosophers as the main argument against extending the franchise to wage-workers. To them the right of voting presupposed economic independence, and as wage-workers were essentially unfree and dependent on others for their livelihood, they were not worthy of being political subjects (Macpherson 1962). This philosophy, however, lost ground as workers and women succeeded in their struggle for universal suffrage. Yet, it remains a fact that the democratic principle only triumphed at the societal level, not at the workplace level.

Some observers have stressed the difference between a direction of labour carried out by the owners or entrepreneurs themselves and one where a group of professional managers is employed to direct the operations of an establishment (Poole 1986a: 40–2). No doubt differences can be found regarding ideology and management methods. Yet, on a general level, it is hardly meaningful to see owners and managers as separate interest groups. Accordingly, in this study, managers are conceived primarily as the representatives of the owners. In general, the terms employer/manager/management will be used synonymously; the few exceptions to this, where managers are seen as a distinct group of employees, will appear from the context. The term 'management', however, will also be used in a different sense: as a technical concept denoting the direction and coordination of the operations of an enterprise – a process in which not only owners and professional managers but also employee-elected representatives may take part.

Historically, the employers' right to manage has not remained unrestricted. It has been challenged in particular by the trade union movement which has succeeded in gaining influence on regulation at workplace level through three partly distinctive, partly overlapping instruments, namely industrial conflict, collective bargaining and participation. At the same time, the powers of employers have been limited through state intervention, i.e. labour legislation and other forms of statutory regulation with a bearing on workplace relations (Rivero Lamas 1986). To varying degrees across countries, state intervention has defined the rights and obligations of employers as well as employees, including employee rights granting influence on management decisions through collective bargaining or participation.

On the basis of different mixes of the above *modes of regulation* at the workplace – unilateral employer decision-making, industrial conflict, collective bargaining, participation and state intervention – a number of different types of *workplace regimes* emerges. The concept of workplace regime is used as an analytical tool; it is inspired by but by no means identical to the factory regimes discussed by Burawoy (1985). In figure 1.3 participation is situated within such a framework.

The model constructed in figure 1.3 takes for granted that workplace industrial relations to some extent are always subject to state regulation which defines the scope and partly also the procedures for the interaction between employers and employees. The question of forms and extent of state intervention is, of course, of great importance (cf. Crouch 1993). Does the state prohibit or promote collective bargaining? Does it grant employee representatives strong participation rights or none at all? Nevertheless, the question of state intervention will be left aside here where the focus is on the relations at workplace level. In the model, participation may be based on state regulation, but it may

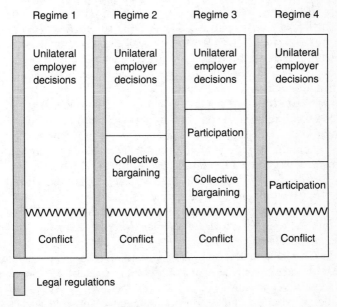

Figure 1.3   *Workplace regimes and modes of regulation*

also result from collective bargaining. Collective bargaining, for its part, may take place at the workplace level as well as at the sector or national level. Another basic assumption behind the model is that conflict, whether manifest or latent, is an inherent feature of workplace industrial relations.

The model distinguishes between four different types of workplace regime. In the *first regime* unilateral employer decisions dominate as the mode of regulation. Formally, employee influence is here limited to the terms fixed in the individual employment contract. Because of the unequal power relations between the two sides, this usually amounts to the employee accepting the wage rate and working hours offered by the employer. The precise quantity and quality of labour to be performed in exchange for the wage remains indeterminate and up to management to define through its orders and its supervision and control over the labour process (Edwards 1979: 12; Littler 1982: 39). In reality, however, employees are never fully without influence over their work situation. Norms for actual performance are defined through a web of informal bargaining processes at the shopfloor level (Brown 1992: 237-8).

Unilateral management rule may be accepted by employees for two reasons. First, they may find it legitimate by seeing it as an expression of a natural or inevitable social order (cf. the deferential worker studied by Lockwood 1958). Secondly, they may lack the power to resist the rules and orders given by management – both the objective power originating from alternative possibilities on the labour market, and the subjective power arising from collective organization (Hyman & Fryer 1975: 162-3; Littler 1982: 44). More typically, however, unilateral management rule will *not* be accepted as a given fact; both individually and collectively, employees will attempt to resist management authority and gain influence over their working conditions. An awareness of distinct interests *vis-à-vis* the employer will lead to conflicts over pay and working conditions. Such conflicts – often experienced by employers as unpredictable and costly – may pave the way for other modes of regulation where the employers attempt to regain control by sharing it, by accommodating to the aspirations of employees and trade unions (Fox 1974; Friedman 1977). This may lead to institutionalized procedures for collective bargaining and participation.

In the *second regime* management rights are limited by collective bargaining. Some writers describe collective bargaining as a form of participation (Merrifierd 1982; Poole 1986a). My own proposition is that it is more adequate to view collective bargaining and participation as distinct ways of representing employee interests and distinct modes of workplace regulation.

Collective bargaining represents a specific and limited type of accommodation to employee interests. It presupposes that a significant number of employees are organized in trade unions and that these are recognized by the state and the employers. Collective bargaining is carried out by a collectivity of employees (usually a trade union) on the one side and an employer or an employers' organization on the other. Agreements reached through this procedure normally run for a specified period of time (typically one or two years) and primarily define some quantitative aspects of the employment relationship, such as pay rates, working hours, special conditions concerning shift-work or overtime work, etc. Traditionally, the more qualitative aspects related to technology, work organization, job content and work performance have not been covered by collective agreements, although the tendency has been for trade unions to broaden the range of subjects negotiated and settled through this procedure.

Collective bargaining does not rule out conflict. Rather, conflict is institutionalized and functions as a potential or real pressure which can be used against the opponent at the negotiating table. Nor does collective bargaining interfere with management rights in the day-to-day running of the workplace. Management has to respect the norms of the collective agreement, but the decision-making structures related to the operations of the workplace remain unchanged.

Collective agreements express compromises over a limited range of issues, and periods of truce within a potentially conflictual relationship. Thus collective bargaining only accomplishes a limited form of accommodation between employer and employee interests. It may strengthen the legitimacy of management, inasmuch as it implies that the collective interests of the employees are to some extent represented in the norms governing the workplace. However, it is not likely to lead to any kind of intensive identification and commitment to company goals among the employees. After all, collective bargaining is firmly based on a zero-sum perspective, and on the notion that the two parties have opposing interests (Littler 1982: 40–1; Crouch 1993: 35–9).

The *third regime* of figure 1.3 represents a further elaboration of combinations of modes of regulation. Here, unilateral employer decision-making and collective bargaining is supplemented by participation. It is difficult to fix a precise borderline between collective bargaining and participation. Within a particular industrial relations system it changes over time, and, as will be shown in following chapters, across nations there may be great variations as to whether a certain issue is dealt with through one or other of these modes of regulation. In relation to collective bargaining, participation – i.e. procedures for information, consultation and co-decision – is both a complementary and a competing way of regulating workplace issues. It is complementary in the sense that participatory decision-making may fill out in detail the frameworks laid down by collective agreement. An example can be working time where the collective agreement may stipulate that normal working hours have to be placed between 6 am and 6 pm on weekdays and that the average working week is 37 hours. It is left to participative decisions at workplace level to define more exactly when work has to be carried out.

More generally, participation complements collective agreements in areas where it is impossible, or at least difficult, to apply collective bargaining as a mode of regulation. Both employers and employees may see an interest in participatory decision-making in relation to processes of change and the day-to-day operations of the establishment. For employers, the gains here will typically consist in a reduction of the uncertainty and unpredictability which always accompany processes of change, and possibly also in a better understanding of, and commitment to, company goals among the workforce (Fröhlich et al. 1991). For employees, participation means a better insight into management decisions and a possible influence over issues which in other workplace regimes are decided by management alone.

But there is also a certain competition between collective bargaining and participation. Trade unions have often preferred collective agreements to consultation and co-decision arrangements because collective bargaining emphasizes the distinct interests of employees, and is closely connected to the conflict weapon. Trade unions may also fear that their members are manipulated through participatory arrangements, or that they develop attitudes where the good of the company becomes more important than the collective interests represented by the union (cf. the German concept of *Betriebsegoismus*). Employers, on the other hand, are usually eager to avoid collective agreements of a very detailed nature which are likely to restrict the flexibility of the workplace and to lead to conflicts over interpretation. Instead, they may be prepared to open up for participatory decision-making as a more cooperative way of solving matters. Some employers view collective bargaining as a too conflictual and inflexible way of accommodating to employee interests and are ready to spend large resources on avoiding this form of regulation altogether. This brings us back to the first regime – or to the *fourth regime* in which unilateral management decision-making is coupled with employee participation, but not collective bargaining.

The problem with this constellation, seen from an employee viewpoint, but also from the viewpoint of efficient regulation, is that the participation of employees is usually based on an extremely unequal distribution of power. Having been able to ensure that workplace regulation takes place without the interference of trade unions and collective agreements, it is not likely that employers will grant employees a real degree of collective influence through participation. This is a fragile basis for participation for, as noted by Lammers & Széll (1989: 324):

> only those processes of participation . . . that imply an increase in power for the participants will tend to become institutionalised. People involved in schemes that do not provide them with a real chance to influence decisions in accordance with their interests or views will obviously not attach much value to such practices, let alone defend them.

Yet, one possibility is to link participation to pecuniary rewards through bonus schemes or profit-sharing. This does not give employees more power at the workplace, but it increases their buying power outside the workplace.

The fourth type has become quite widespread in the US and, with some modifications, in Japan. It can also be found to some extent in Britain, where, however, the first and second regimes are more typical. Contrary to this, the third regime is predominant in Denmark, Germany, Spain and other continental EU member states, although the concrete mix of unilateralism, conflict, collective bargaining and participation varies a great deal, both among and within these countries. Moreover, the countries differ as to whether participation is primarily a mode of regulation in a formal sense or also in a real sense, a theme which will be pursued in the following chapters. The classification of countries above is based on formal considerations, i.e. industrial relations rules rather than practices.

Again, in this context it must be stressed that there is no 'natural' or objective space for participation. For participation to become rooted within workplace regimes it requires:

- that both parties recognize each other as parties with legitimate but also diverging interests; this implies, for example, that employees view the prosperity of the company as important, while conversely employers see the job security and well-being of employees as important;
- that both parties experience gains from moving away from an essentially conflictual zero-sum logic and in the direction of a cooperation concerning the creation and distribution of new plus-sums;
- that the relations between the parties are characterized by trust (Fox 1974); i.e. that one party can feel secure that the other party will not attempt to appropriate all the gains stemming from a common effort.

Such conditions are not easily established and maintained in capitalist workplaces. For systemic as well as opportunistic and ideological reasons, the behaviour of the parties is often governed by a desire to get as much as possible here and now. In this connection, the national systems of regulation of industrial relations play an important role in conditioning workplace relations. As pointed out by Crouch (1993), who distinguishes between *contestation, pluralist bargaining* and *bargained corporatism* as qualitatively different forms of regulation and exchange, bargained corporatism (which is predominant in Germany and Denmark among the countries selected for this study) is the form which not only gives labour the strongest position, but also the only one which systematically stimulates workplace relations of a cooperative character.

If some of the arguments made so far appear rather abstract, it is hoped that they will become both more intelligible and more convincing through the country profiles presented in chapters 2–5. But first I must briefly introduce the theme of national diversity versus international convergence.

Convergence between national participation systems?

It has been a central objective of my study not just to attempt to explain how and why participation structures vary from one EU country to the other, but also to identify socioeconomic and political forces with a possible common impact on all the countries. An essential question in this respect has been whether there are trends towards convergence between the EU countries as far as the forms and the intensity of employee participation is concerned. Are there factors of a global and/or European nature which tend to eradicate existing national diversities and to create uniformity across the member states? From a theoretical perspective there are good reasons to expect convergence to have taken place and/or to take place in the future within an area such as employee participation.

In Marxist theory, it is a fundamental assumption that the mode of production (relations between owners and producers, and the forms of organization and technique used in economic activities) conditions all social relations and institutions within a given society. In some versions, the theory claims a simple deterministic relationship between base (the economy) and superstructure (law, political, social and cultural institutions). Other variants are more open-ended and tend to put the emphasis on the interdependence or congruence between changes within the different spheres of society (see e.g. Thompson 1978; Gouldner 1980). In any event, a Marxist perspective would suggest that such changes in the mode of production as technological innovation, the internationalization of trade and property relations, and the integration of national economies within the European Union, will be accompanied by related changes in social institutions, for instance institutions for employee participation.

Among studies directed at the subject of European integration, the neo-functionalist theory has played an influential role. Briefly stated, the theory maintains that integration within one sector of the economy will lead to pressures for integration in other sectors as well, through what is termed functional spillover effects. It also envisages political spillovers, i.e. changes in political and social institutions related to economic integration. The theory has had its setbacks, in close connection to the setbacks to European integration experienced especially between the mid-1970s and the mid-1980s. However, it has now gained renewed credibility, in particular in reformulated versions which combine the notion of a supranational integration dynamic with an acknowledgement of the existence of nationalist policies which pull in the opposite direction (George 1991). Not least because the institutions for employee participation at workplace level are intimately related to the economy – indeed, in a sense they are part of economic organizations – the neo-functionalist theory implicitly supports the expectation that economic integration will be accompanied by some kind of harmonization or convergence within employee participation.

Finally, a point of reference can be found in the theory of convergence proposed by Kerr et al. (1962). This theory points to 'industrialism' as a factor which will lead to the gradual, although hardly complete, convergence of political and social institutions across national borders. This will occur irrespective of prior diversities, and even between societies organized along the principles of private capitalism and state socialism respectively. Although the theory recognizes a number of forces working against convergence – among them the inertia of already established institutions tending 'to develop a life of its own' (1962: 279) – it states on the general level that 'the industrial system tends to develop a common set of rules under common technological and economic conditions. Cultural and national differences are less significant to the web of rules, the further a country is along the road towards industrialism' (1962: 42). The central driving forces in industrial societies are defined as science, technology and production methods; and these are claimed to 'have a number of decisive consequences for workers, managers, the state, and their interrelation' (1962: 34). Technology especially is emphasized as a factor creating global uniformity, one specific thesis being that 'social arrangements will be most uniform from one society to another when they are most closely tied to technology; they can be more diverse the farther they are removed from technology' (1962: 285).

In 1983 Kerr published a revised version of the theory of convergence. In this he attempted to demonstrate that convergence has gone farthest in the areas of knowledge, mobilization of the factors of production, organization of production, patterns of work and living, and patterns of distribution of economic rewards. On the other hand, diversity has shown its persistence in areas such as economic structures, political structures, religious beliefs, national identities, and highest-priority social goals (Kerr 1983: 73). He also contended – without giving any empirical evidence – that 'there now seems to be some nearly universal trends toward more emphasis on . . . more participation in workplace decisions' (1983: 54–5).

Kerr's theory has also had its setbacks, notably related to the decades of seeming immutability in Eastern Europe and the former Soviet Union. However, the capitalist revolutions in this part of the world since 1989 may be interpreted as its belated, but great triumph. Yet, the convergence unleashed by these revolutions has not been of the gradual, evolutionary character predicted by the theory. Moreover, there are many speculations as to whether these changes were caused mainly by 'industrial society', 'information society' or some third set of factors. (I will abstain from commenting further on the different theories on 'information society'. In my view, information technology has led to a new phase in the development of capitalism and industry, not to a qualitatively new type of society. Consequently, I consider neither Marxist theory nor the convergence theory of Kerr et al. to be outdated.)

For the purposes of my own analyses of employee participation, the most interesting aspect of Kerr's theory is the contention that changes in economic and, especially, technological conditions act as forces leading to a greater transnational uniformity in social arrangements. This once again suggests that diverse national arrangements for employee participation will tend to become more uniform over time.

In spite of having different objectives and basic assumptions, all the three theories presented above lend support to the realism of the notion of a specific European model for employee participation. Economic and technological changes of a global nature, as well as economic and political changes specific to the EU, generally speak for convergence, and thus implicitly also within the particular area of employee participation in management decisions. The question of convergence is a central theme of this book and will be taken up in chapters 6–8.

But first we shall look at the development of participation in a national perspective. Chapters 2–5 portray the participation systems, seen as subsystems of the total industrial relations system, of four different EU member states.

2

Germany: Participation Based on
Strong Legal Rights

The German industrial relations system is often described as legalistic because of the existence of relatively comprehensive and detailed legal norms for the behaviour of the social actors of the system. Labour legislation has had as its goal to regulate social conflict and to harmonize social interests, but also to delimit state interference by defining a distinct autonomous space for employers and employees, and their respective organizations. The underlying philosophy is that the state, after having constructed a legal framework, should refrain from intervening in industrial relations issues (Endruweit & Berger 1986: 125).

The representation of the interests of German employees takes place through a dual channel system where formally there is a clear demarcation and division of labour between trade unions and collective bargaining on the one side, and workplace representatives and enterprise-related activities on the other. Collective bargaining is performed for the different sectors or industries at state (*Land*) or federal level. The parties are trade unions and employers' organizations or single employers. The collective agreements apply to all enterprises within the bargaining unit in question. Contrary to collective bargaining, the representation and participation at enterprise level is defined as in principle lying outside the scope of the trade unions. Here, the collective interests of the employees are expressed by the works council – elected by all employees irrespective of trade union affiliation – and through employee representatives on the supervisory board.

The great majority of organized German workers are affiliated to the confederation Deutscher Gewerkschaftsbund (DGB). By 1992 total trade union membership was just around 40 per cent, and 34 per cent of the labour force belonged to trade unions affiliated to the DGB. German unification meant that a slowly decreasing trade union density in West Germany, down to 37 per cent prior to unification, was more than offset by a high density in the former East Germany (Lecher 1994: 162).

The German industrial relations system has attracted much interest internationally (Schregle 1978: 81). The main reason for this has been the German *Wirtschaftswunder* since the war and the fact that economic and technological efficiency has co-existed with, and probably been increased by, industrial peace and relatively advanced forms of employee participation. A 'happy' combination which only seriously began to be challenged by the strains caused by German unification and the economic crisis of the early 1990s.

Historical outline

The backbone of German employee participation is the works council (*Betriebsrat*). This type of body was advocated by liberal employers and reformist bourgeois politicians in the last part of the nineteenth century. At that time German trade unions were opposed to such institutions because they were seen as a threat to trade union unity and – as expressed by the Social Democratic leader August Bebel – as a 'figleaf of capitalism' (Müller-Jentsch 1986: 217).

The state showed its interest in cooperative workplace bodies in 1891 when a law on labour protection made it optional to establish works committees (*Arbeiterausschüsse*). In 1905 works committees were made obligatory in the mining industry, in the wake of a major strike, and during the First World War, an act extended the provision of such bodies to all factories with more than 50 employees in industries of basic importance for the war economy (Fürstenberg 1978: 1).

After the war, the German labour movement was in a strong position, but divided between a radical wing which wanted to take power in the factories through workers councils (like the Soviets in Russia), and a reformist wing with a strategy based on trade union and parliamentary activity. Confronted by the revolutionary threat, the big industrialists moved closer to the reformist trade unions, and for the first time acknowledged them as representative bargaining partners, a recognition which shortly after was followed by the government (Müller-Jentsch 1986: 218–19).

The aspirations of the radical part of the labour movement were disappointed by the adoption of the Act on works councils (*Betriebsrätegesetz*) in 1920. Although a concession in form, this law in content left no autonomous power to the workers councils. On the contrary, it codified the still existing dual loyalty of the works councils by defining their functions as 'representing the interests of the workers' and 'supporting the employer in the fulfilment of the goals of the enterprise'. The cooperative character of the works council was further underlined by a peace obligation (Müller-Jentsch 1986: 218).

In 1922 the law was supplemented by an act providing for the (minority) representation of works councillors on the supervisory board of the company (Fürstenberg 1978: 2). The main features of the German industrial relations system had been established: regulation through collective bargaining on the levels above the single firm, regulation through works councils and representatives on the supervisory board at firm level. The continuity, however, was broken by the Hitler regime which suppressed the activities of trade unions as well as works councils and introduced strictly authoritarian relations through the Gesetz zur Ordnung der nationalen Arbeit from 1934 (Müller-Jentsch 1986: 219).

Although the dominant part of the trade union movement had sided with 'the establishment' in the turbulent years after the First World War, it was not satisfied with the results of its compromise with the bourgeois forces. In 1928 the German trade union confederation adopted a programme on economic democracy aiming at co-determination through the three different channels of works councils, trade unions and labour market legislation. These ideas survived Hitler and were guidelines for the demands put forward during the reorganization of German society after the Second World War. The goal was formulated as creating equality between capital and labour.

In the immediate post-war years the trade unions were in a strong position due to the collapse of the Nazi power structures, and to the fact that leading industrialists had been compromised by their collaboration with Hitler (Schmidt 1971). There was a widespread consensus, both within Germany and among the occupying countries, that the big trusts should never again be allowed to dominate the German economy. In 1947 an agreement was reached between the trade unions and the British military government giving the trade union side a parity representation on the supervisory boards in the iron and steel producing companies and a right to appoint a 'labour director' as an equal member of the management of the firms.

The works councils were revitalized through a framework law passed in 1946 by the Allied Control Council. The law stipulated, in the Anglo-Saxon tradition, that works councils could be established and their functions determined on the basis of negotiations between trade unions and employers. The following year the trade unions formulated their demands to the works councils. These should give employees and the employer equal rights in relation to decisions on type of production, investments, work methods, price policy, etc. – in short, co-decision on all important questions. All these rights should be exercised under the leadership of the trade unions, and the works councils should operate as trade union bodies in order to make them less dependent on pressure from the management. During 1947 and 1948 some of the regions (*Länder*) passed legislation which was favourable to trade union demands, but some of the more far-reaching provisions were overruled by the military governments, of which the American was particularly opposed to granting extended powers to trade unions.

In 1949 the new (West) Germany became a reality, and the first elections resulted in a CDU/CSU dominated coalition government. The government tried to change the co-determination arrangement of the iron and steel producing industries but, threatened by a strike call backed by a referendum among the workers, it gave way and passed a law in 1951 on co-determination in the iron, steel and mining industries where the extensive economic participation rights were upheld.

After prolonged negotiations between the government, the trade unions and the employers' organizations, a new law on works councils, the Works Constitution Act (Betriebsverfassungsgesetz) was passed in 1952. The DGB called this event 'a black day in the democratic development of the Federal Republic' (Schmidt 1971: 220). The law did not give the works councils any co-decision rights over financial and production issues, it only granted the employees one-third of the seats on the supervisory boards, and it excluded employees in the public sector. It was not until 1995 that a federal law on participation for the public sector was enacted. It was supplemented by similar laws in the individual regions (Federal Minister 1980: 10; Weiss 1986: 56).

Under the Social Democrat/Liberal coalition government of the 1970s the trade union side managed to improve the participation rights of employees to a certain degree, partly through a revised Works Constitution Act passed in 1972, and partly through the Act on Workers' Co-determination (Mitbestimmungsgesetz) from 1976 (Fürstenberg 1978: 2–3). The latter improved the representation of employees on the supervisory boards of undertakings employing more than 2,000 persons. A revision of the Works Constitution Act introduced in 1989 by the CDU/CSU/FDP government only contained some changes of minor importance.

Institutionalized participation in private firms in Germany today is thus based on three different laws, namely the Act on Co-determination in the iron, steel and mining industry (1951), the Works Constitution Act (1951/1972/1989), and the Co-determination Act (1976). The following sections will go deeper into the norms and practices of the institutions regulated by these laws.

Works councils: the legal provisions

The German works councils are unitary bodies representing all employees except for management staff and are formally independent of both trade unions and employers. The works council meets with the employer at least once a month. Any firm which has at least five employees is required to establish a works council, and elections take place every four years. Within this period, the works councillors cannot be recalled by the employees; only a labour court decision can remove

Table 2.1 *Number of works councillors according to workforce size in Germany*

Size of workforce	No. of works councillors
5–20	1
21–50	3
51–150	5
151–300	7
301–600	9
601–1000	11
1001–2000	15
2001–3000	19
3001–4000	23
4001–5000	27
5001–7000	29
7001–9000	31
9000+	2 extra for every additional fraction of 3000

them from office. For elections, employees are normally divided into a blue-collar and a white-collar group, but candidate lists can cover both groups. The number of works councillors to be elected varies with the size of the workforce (see table 2.1).

The works council system is primarily plant based. However, when a company has several plants, the works council from each plant can appoint delegates to a central works council – and in groups of companies to a group works council.

As stated in art. 2 and art. 80 of the Works Constitution Act (Federal Minister 1980: 96–192), the works councils have the dual function of working 'for the good of the employees and of the establishment'. In the following we shall look closer at the rights, obligations, facilities and protections accorded to the works councils and their members.

Information rights   The Works Constitution Act states as a general duty for the employer to 'supply comprehensive information to the works council in good time' and to grant 'access at any time to any documentation it may require for the discharge of its duties' (art. 80). This duty to inform is further specified, particularly in relation to financial matters and alterations in production and work processes.

In companies with more than 20 employees, the works council has a right to receive information on 'alterations which may entail substantial prejudice to the staff or a large sector thereof' (art. 111). More specifically, the following types of changes are mentioned: reduction of operations, partial closures, transfers of departments, amalgamations, important organizational or technical changes, introduction of new work methods and production processes.

In companies with more than 100 employees the works council must appoint a finance committee (*Wirtschaftsausschuss*). This committee meets once a month with the management and is entitled to obtain information on the following subjects:

- the financial, production and marketing situation of the company;
- production and investment programmes and rationalization plans;
- production techniques and work methods;
- the reduction of operations, the full or partial closure of plants, the transfer and amalgamation of plants;
- changes in the organization and objectives of the enterprise;
- and 'any other circumstances and projects that may materially affect the interests of the employees' (art. 106).

Information on 'the financial situation and progress of the company' must also be given directly to the employees, at least in firms with more than 20 workers. For enterprises with over 1,000 employees the information must be in writing and be given at least quarterly (art. 110).

As will appear from the following, some of the information rights can lead on to consultations, negotiations or even co-decisions.

Consultation rights   The works council is empowered to be informed and consulted on any plans concerning the construction or alteration of work buildings, the technical plant, the work process and work operations, and the jobs (art. 90). This must happen with regard to the 'established findings of ergonomics relating to the tailoring of jobs to meet human requirements'. In an amendment of the law in 1989 it was stressed that the information and consultation shall take place at an early stage, so that proposals from the works council may be able to influence planning.

Consultation is also envisaged in relation to manpower planning (art. 92), matters related to staff training (arts 96, 97) and before dismissals (art. 102) (Schneider 1989: 396). Finally, the finance committee has a right, and even a duty, to consultation on financial matters (art. 106).

Bearing in mind that consultation is not co-decision, it is nevertheless noteworthy that the works council (or the finance committee) is entitled to express its views on all important tactical decisions of the enterprise.

Co-decision rights   In a number of areas the works council has a co-decision right. This means that management cannot take any decisions without the consent of the works council, or, if it does, that the decision may be declared illegal by the labour court. If the employer and the works council cannot agree on a specific co-decision issue, the matter is referred to a conciliation committee (*Einigungsstelle*) consisting of an equal number of members chosen by the works council and the employer, and a chairman appointed by both parties in common. The decision of the conciliation committee is binding, unless one of the parties is able to get it changed through a labour court decision. Co-decisions – taken directly between the parties or, more seldom, by the conciliation committee – often take the form of a works agreement (*Betriebsvereinbarung*). Works agreements can cover any issue which is not fixed by a collective agreement (art. 77).

Co-decision applies to the following 'social' issues mentioned in art. 87 of the Works Constitution Act:

- rules of order and conduct in the enterprise;
- the commencement and termination of daily working hours and breaks, and the distribution of working hours among the days of the week;
- temporary reductions or extensions of the normal working time;
- principles for holiday arrangements and holiday schedules;
- technical devices for monitoring the performance or behaviour of the employees;
- the protection of health and the prevention of employment accidents and occupational diseases;
- the administration of company-based social services;
- the administration of accommodation rented to employees;
- principles of remuneration and the introduction of new payment systems;
- the fixing of job and bonus rates and performance-related remuneration.

A particular co-decision right is prescribed for cases where the employer changes working conditions in obvious contradiction to the established findings of ergonomics 'relating to the tailoring of jobs to meet human requirements' (art. 91). If the employer is not willing to meet the demands of the works council on improving the conditions, or to compensate for their negative effects, the conciliation committee shall decide on the matter.

Further co-decision rights exist within the area of personnel questions: regarding staff questionnaires and personal data contained in written employment contracts (art. 94), guidelines for the selection of employees for recruitment, transfer, regrading and dismissal (art. 95), the implementation of vocational training programmes, i.e. the appointment of training officers and the selection of employees for training (art. 98).

Finally, the works councils in firms with more than 20 employees have a right to negotiate on 'alterations which may entail substantial prejudice to the staff' (rationalization measures), and a co-decision right as to the consequences of such changes. Here it is envisaged that management negotiates a 'social compensation plan' (*Sozialplan*) with the works council. If no agreement is reached, the question will be settled by the conciliation committee which must 'take into account the social interests of the employees concerned while taking care that its decision does not place an unreasonable financial burden on the company' (art. 112). Seen in relation to the traditional German distinction between social, personnel and financial matters as three different areas for participation, the social compensation plan is the only case of co-decision within the financial area.

Veto rights   In a few areas the works council is actually empowered to block the decision of the employer. If an employer employs, grades, regrades or transfers an employee in breach of labour legislation, a collective agreement or the locally agreed guidelines, the works council 'may refuse its consent' (art. 99). In order to go ahead with the decision, the employer must take the case before the labour court – and win it. Similarly, the works council can object to a dismissal if 'social considerations' have not been taken, if the dismissed could be 'kept on at another job' or kept on through retraining or through a 'change in terms of his contract' (art. 102). An objection from the works council, combined with an appeal to the labour court by the dismissed worker, can oblige the employer to 'keep the employee in his employment . . . until a final decision is given on the case'.

Peace obligation   The works council is not allowed to call strikes or take industrial action of any kind to further its goals. The Works Constitution Act states that 'acts of industrial warfare between the employer and the works council shall be unlawful' (art. 74). The significance of the peace obligation is great. Instead of being able to rely on collective action, the works council must always take the position of the third party (the conciliation committee or the labour court) into account when using its co-decision powers. This is indeed a moderating factor, tending to prevent radical demands and grievances and to promote tactics for gaining only piecemeal concessions.

Obligations towards the employer   The works council must work together with the employer 'in a spirit of mutual trust' (art. 2) and is expected to take part in the maintenance of social stability and order in the enterprise. One example of the disciplinary functions of the works council is its explicitly mentioned right of initiative in cases where 'an

employee . . . repeatedly causes serious trouble in the establishment'
(art. 104).

All members and substitute members are obliged to keep a professional secrecy in relation to 'trade or business secrets . . . which the
employer has expressly stated to be confidential' (art. 79).

Facilities and protection   The works council is entitled to meet during
working hours (art. 30). The expenses arising from its activities are
carried by the employer who is also obliged to provide 'the premises,
material facilities and office staff required for . . . the operation of the
works council' (art. 40). The members of the works council have a
right to be released from their work duties without loss of pay for the
time necessary for performing their function. In enterprises with more
than 300 employees, one or more of the representatives can be released
full time (ranging from one in enterprises with between 300 and 600
employees, to 11 where the workforce is between 9,000 and 10,000
employees) (arts 37 and 38). Part of the time off can be used for attend-
ing training courses.

As for protection against dismissal, art. 78 simply states that works
council members 'shall not be prejudiced or favoured by reason of
their office'. Contrary to this, the Act on Protection against Dismissal
stipulates that a works council member, or a candidate for works council elections, cannot be dismissed unless the person in question has
committed such a grave offence that the employer is justified in dis-
missing the person without notice. In cases where a department is
closed down, works council members employed there are entitled to be
transferred to another department, if it is possible 'for operational reasons' (Federal Minister 1980: 182–3).

Communication between works council and employees   The individual
worker may contact the works council during its consultation hours,
without loss of pay, and may ask the works council to forward grievances and suggestions.

Once every quarter the works council shall call a works meeting or
department meeting in order to report on its activities (art. 42–6). The
meetings are not public, but are open to the employer and to trade
unions represented in the enterprise. The meetings can make suggestions to the works council, take a stand on its decisions, and can also
discuss questions in connection with collective bargaining. Meetings
are held during work hours and without loss of pay. Empirical studies,
however, show that four works meetings per year is the exception rather
than the rule; in most plants meetings are held less frequently if at all
(Weiss 1987: 155).

The works councils in practice

So far, only the formal rules governing the activities of the works councils have been presented. But what about practice? Do the councils
function in accordance with the prescribed norms?

In some enterprises they do not function at all. It has been shown
that works councils exist in only 6 per cent of enterprises with between
five and 20 employees (Biagi 1993: 848). Weiss (1987: 150) states that
only around 20 per cent of all plants required to establish a works
council have actually done so, the large enterprises being the only ones
to comply fully with the law. Nevertheless, a majority of German
employees is covered by a works council. According to statistics from
the DGB there was a considerable rise in the number of works councils
during the 1960s and 1970s, but from 1981 to 1990 the number of
councils fell from 36,300 to 33,000 and the corresponding number of
councillors declined from 199,100 to 183,700.

In a major study on the influence of works councils, it was found that
their ability to represent the interests of employees effectively, corresponded positively with workforce size and trade union presence (shop
stewards) in the establishment, and negatively with the personal intervention of the owner in the social relations of the firm. The study (in
which medium-sized enterprises were over-represented) found that the
participation of the works council seen from an employee perspective
was only successful in 35 per cent of the enterprises, while in 65 per cent
of the cases the works council was either isolated, ignored or simply
functioned as an instrument for management (Müller-Jentsch 1986:
226–7). Another study, dealing with technical and organizational
changes in the metal industry, found that the works councils were not
active partners in initiating, planning and designing change. This was
ascribed to a combination of a restrictive information policy on the
part of managers, a lack of professional technical knowledge among
works councillors, and the fact that participation rights are relatively
weak in relation to the technical and organizational design of work
processes (Müller-Jentsch 1986: 227).

On the other hand, there is evidence of works councils being able to
gain concessions in areas where they formally have little influence, by
combining different issues in the negotiations with management. An
example is when employers want to introduce overtime work. Here, the
employer must obtain the consent of the works council, or bear the
risk, and loss of time, involved in a conciliation. The works council can
use its position of strength to obtain a 'package deal' where it accepts
overtime work, while the employer in return gives concessions on other
issues (Thüssing 1986: 164; Visser 1993: 816).

As for the other part of their dual function – to work 'for the good of the establishment' – it is generally recognized that the works councils are doing well (Fürstenberg 1978: 14–15; Schregle 1978: 86–7; Martens 1992: 37). In some cases, the activities of the works council have obvious advantages for management; for example, regarding the administration of social welfare services and the selection of workers for dismissals. In general, the buffer status of the works council between management and employees helps to minimize conflicts and to facilitate acceptance of management decisions. On the other hand, it is also true that the works council constitutes a direct cost for the enterprise and that indirect costs may result from the restrictions put on management's ability to act here and now (Thüssing 1986: 164).

On the whole, the works councils have proved able to promote a high degree of social integration at workplace level by balancing their representation and their participation or cooperation functions. This has been done, however, without interfering with the traditional hard core of management decisions: the strategic decisions of major financial, technological and organizational importance. And, on the whole, their role has remained reactive towards management initiatives.

However, in recent years there have been tendencies for works councils to take a more active part in the dynamic development of enterprises, at least in the more advanced sectors of industry and service. When managements have tried to improve productivity by technological, organizational and motivational changes, the works councils have attempted not only to get the best out of it in terms of employment protection, payment etc., but also to influence the whole process of change by putting forward qualitative demands related to the structuring and content of work. As a consequence, the cooperation between works councils and management has been intensified, at the same time as the area for potential conflict has been widened (Kern & Schumann 1985: 117–37; Sperling 1991: 69). Changes in management policies (implying a greater involvement of workers) as well as reformulations of trade union strategies have made it urgent for works councils to become engaged in management decisions in a more proactive way.

Relations between works councils and trade unions

As already mentioned, the German trade unions were critical of the Works Constitution Act of 1952, one of the reasons being that the law excluded the trade unions from any formal influence over the works councils. This situation was improved somewhat with the revision of the law in 1972 which allowed trade union officials to attend works council and works meetings and to have access to the establishments in general. Still, the works councils remain formally non-union organizations and hold a monopoly over functions which in other industrial relations systems are fulfilled by the unions.

The trade unions have responded to this situation by developing two different ways of attempting to gain influence at plant level. The first way has been to further the election of shop stewards (*Vertrauensleute*) who, as alternative representatives, may put pressure on the works council. The second way has consisted in trying to control the works council by putting up candidates at the elections and influencing the activities of the works council. In general, the shop stewards have not been able to compete with the powers of the works council – rather they have been subordinated to the activities of the latter (Streeck 1984: 28–30; Zoll 1991: 216–18). The second method has been more successful. In spite of the fact that only about a third of wage-earners is organized in the DGB trade unions, candidates from these unions fill a clear majority of the works council seats (Jacobi & Müller-Jentsch 1990: 134). The works council elections of 1994 resulted in 66.7 per cent of the seats going to unions affiliated to the DGB, 6.8 per cent to members of other unions, while 26.5 per cent went to unorganized employees (EIRR 1994b: 7). This means, given the fact that German unions are industrial unions following the principle of 'one plant, one union', that most works councils in reality function as the basic unit of trade union organization, as 'the prolonged arm of the union movement' (Schregle 1986: 180).

The relations between trade unions and works councils are characterized by mutual dependence and support. The trade union depends on the works council to have its collective agreements implemented in the workplace, to have its policies propagated, to recruit members etc. And the works council for its part depends on the union in relation to training, professional expertise and assistance in working out proposals for works agreements.

Since the 1970s plant-level agreements (work councils) have gained in relative importance compared to collective bargaining (the trade union) (Endruweit & Berger 1986: 138). At first this was a result of trade union policies for furthering 'qualitative' demands on work organization, new technology, job content etc. – demands which can be promoted in a general form through collective bargaining, but has to be followed up by specific agreements at workplace level in order to be implemented. From the 1980s, the employers' organizations have increasingly insisted on a decentralization of the settling of issues. Thus, as an example, the trade union struggle for a 35 hour week resulted in a series of compromises where the unions obtained a reduction of working hours, but only on the condition that the regulation of working time became more flexible; it was left to the enterprises and works councils to decide how the reduction should be implemented for different groups of employees (Endruweit & Berger 1986: 136–7; Sperling 1991: 68).

These tendencies for qualitative demands and decentralization of decisions mean that collective bargaining increasingly takes the form of framework agreements. It also implies that the functions of the works council may become more comprehensive and more offensive. As an example, the 1987 technology agreement between IG Metall and Volkswagen gave the works council a right to be informed and consulted during the planning of technological changes, and it obliged the management to develop qualification programmes in cooperation with the works council (Sperling 1991: 69). This and similar agreements which extend the scope of the participation of works councils indicate that these bodies are gaining in importance on the *basis* of offensive trade union policies. In other cases, decentralization rather seems to strengthen the works councils at the *expense* of, if not the trade unions, at least those types of solidaristic solutions that trade unions have traditionally stood for.

Co-determination on the supervisory boards

During the reorganization of German society after the Second World War, one of the most important trade union demands was equality between capital and labour in all decisions having to do with the economy, including the important production and investment decisions of individual firms. At that time, the DGB put more emphasis on the demand for parity representation on the company boards than on co-decision rights in relation to the day-to-day management of the workplace (Schregle 1986: 178).

Since then, trade union priorities have changed gradually. In 1965 the slogan 'co-determination at the workplace' was included in the programme of the DGB, and some headway in this respect was made by the revision of the Works Constitution Act in 1972 where the degree of influence on a number of issues was changed from consultation to co-decision. Nevertheless, co-determination at *board level* has been and remains a central feature of the German participation system. Co-determination rests on three different legal regulations:

1   The most far-reaching co-determination exists in the mining and iron and steel producing industries, the *Montanindustrie*, according to the above-mentioned law from 1951, Gesetz über die Mitbestimmung der Arbeitnehmer in den Aufsichtsräten und Vorständen der Unternehmen des Bergbaues und der Eisen- und Stahlerzeugenden Industrie (Federal Minister 1980: 73–92). It grants employees a representation equal to that of the owners on the supervisory board (usually 5 + 5), with an additional 'neutral'

person being appointed by owner and employee representatives in common. The employee side consists of two representatives elected by the employees of the firm and three trade union representatives. The law also provides for the election of a 'labour director' (*Arbeitsdirektor*) who has a position equal to the other, usually two, directors on the management board (*Vorstandsrat*). This person cannot be appointed against the wishes of the majority of the employee representatives on the supervisory board.

2   A weaker form of participation on the supervisory board is regulated through the Mitbestimmungsgesetz of 1976 covering firms with more than 2,000 employees (Federal Minister 1980: 7–73). Although formally granting parity representation, the law stipulates that the chairman (usually a representative of the owners) has two votes in situations where there is a tie. Furthermore, the law demands that one of the employee representatives must be elected among management staff. From a trade union point of view it is also a weakness that the labour director here can be appointed against the votes of a majority of the employee representatives.

3   Finally, for companies with between 500 and 2,000 employees the provisions of the Works Constitution Act of 1952 are still in force. This act determines that one-third of the members of the supervisory board shall be employee representatives (Federal Minister 1980: 93–9). The labour director institution is not included in this law.

Of these different forms of participation at board level, the first covers some 20 companies employing about half a million workers; the second some 500 companies with approximately 4.5 million workers; while the third form is relevant for around one million employees (Müller-Jentsch 1986: 233).

What is the experience with the far-reaching co-determination which has existed since 1951 in the *Montanindustrie*? First of all, the relations between the two sides have been characterized by cooperation rather than conflict. Out-voting has been rare and the 'neutral' members have not exerted a major influence, but have functioned mainly as mediators (Fürstenberg 1978: 24). It is remarkable that a cooperative spirit has been predominant even though the sector has constantly been in decline and gone through a long series of rationalizations and closures. The cooperation has fundamentally been based on an exchange, where employee representatives have accepted traditional management criteria in financial and production issues at the same time as they have obtained concessions in the social area, in relation to redundancy payment, the re-employment of workers in other jobs, etc. (Fürstenberg 1978: 24–30). On the basis of this exchange, the shrinking of the

German coal and steel industry has taken place without major confrontations between capital and labour – contrary to what has been the
case in, for instance, France and Britain.

Similarly, the existence of labour directors has not led to any fundamental changes in management practice. Labour directors are usually
in charge of social policies and personnel administration and in this
respect they have played an important role in developing modern,
employee-friendly personnel management styles. But, in general, labour
directors are true to their acquired management identity rather than
their labour background; they feel responsible towards joint management decisions and are ready to defend them when confronted with
employee demands in bargaining situations. This company loyalty on
the part of employee representatives in the management is usually fully
accepted by the trade unions (Schregle 1986: 179).

It goes without saying that the two other and weaker forms of
employee participation on the supervisory board have had a smaller
impact on company practices than the *Montanindustrie* regulation. In
general, participation through the supervisory and management boards
has changed neither the economic logic nor the basic priorities followed by companies; it has, however, furthered cooperative relations
between the two parties, prevented conflicts over rationalizations, and
helped to develop social and personnel policies to the advantage of
employees (Kissler 1989: 85–6).

Other forms of employee participation

Shop stewards   Most German trade unions have provisions for the
election of shop stewards (*Vertrauensleute*) in the single departments or
shops of the enterprises. However, neither the state nor the employers'
organizations have been interested in promoting this type of employee
representation, given the existence of the works council institution.
Legislation is silent on shop stewards, and collective agreements in
general limit themselves to stating that the employers acknowledge
their existence and guarantee against discrimination against them
(Müller-Jentsch 1986: 198–200). Trade union attempts to extend some
of the privileges of the works councillors (paid time off for meetings
etc.) to the shop stewards have not been successful, and shop stewards
enjoy no formal rights to participate in management decisions.

Safety delegates and committees   The German legal regulation on
health and safety has since 1963 provided for the appointment of
employee safety delegates within the enterprises; and, since 1973, a
safety committee, composed of employer and worker representatives
and professional experts, has been mandatory in those enterprises

which are required by law to employ health and safety experts (Gevers 1983: 414–18). However, the powers of the safety delegates and the safety committees are limited to monitoring and consultative functions, the works council being the primary body for the representation and participation of employees in health and safety matters.

As already mentioned, the works council has a co-decision right in relation to the protection of health and the prevention of employment accidents and occupational diseases as well as consultation rights regarding changes with an impact on working conditions. A study of the functioning of works councils in the health and safety area indicates that in practice co-decision is exercised in a relatively defensive way, influence being focused on the selection and functioning of professional experts rather than on technical matters (Gevers 1983: 421).

Managers' committees   In 1989 a law was passed which introduced provisions for the establishment of a management committee *(Sprecherausschuss)*. This committee gives managers the opportunity to consult with top management on a number of issues (Schneider 1989: 397–8).

New technology and participation

As first pointed out by Kern and Schumann (1985), significant sectors of German industry have developed new production concepts in order to cope successfully with structural changes such as sharpened international competition, the need for greater flexibility in the face of rapidly changing market conditions, and the new processes and products made possible by the introduction of new information and communication technologies. Central to the new production concepts is the high priority given to the skills and motivation of the workers as well as their ability to act as a cooperating and responsible collective. New technology, thus, has been one of the factors inducing enlightened managers to extend and intensify cooperation with the workforce, partly through the establishment of direct forms of participation, such as semi-autonomous workgroups and quality circles, and partly through the institutions for indirect employee participation, notably the works councils. Conversely, the works council system has contributed to the fact that technological change has been a relatively conflict-free issue in Germany.

At the same time, trade union strategies towards new technology have become more offensive. While technology agreements in the 1970s were typically limited to a regulation of the social consequences of new technology (employment protection etc.), union demands, and the ensuing agreements, from the mid-1980s have focused increasingly on participation in the implementation of new techniques, the design of jobs and work organization, and the development of qualifications (Weiss 1989: 133; Sperling 1991: 69). In 1988, while the government was preparing an amendment to the Works Constitution Act, the trade unions pressed for full co-decision rights in relation to the introduction of new technology.

While earlier being sceptical, or even hostile, towards direct participation, the DGB unions have since 1984 pursued a consensual line towards this issue and are now eager to negotiate framework agreements which leave it to the works councils to enter into more specific agreements at plant level (Endruweit & Berger 1986: 136; Sperling 1991: 70–1). In several cases agreements have been reached between management and the works council on schemes for direct participation, specifying procedures and the role of the works councils; in other cases, though, management has introduced such schemes unilaterally (Müller-Jentsch et al. 1992: 103).

The consequence of these changes in management as well as trade union policies has been a significant growth in the functions of the works councils. Although concluded in only a minority of companies, works agreements increasingly include the planning of technical and work organizational changes, the design of jobs, and the development of training programmes based on a balancing of employee and management priorities. These new issues put great demands on the works councillors as far as professional knowledge is concerned – demands which the trade unions attempt to meet through training activities and expert assistance (Sperling 1991: 72).

All in all, new technologies, or rather the strategies followed by management and trade unions in relation to these, have led to a higher degree of autonomy of works councils *vis-à-vis* trade unions and collective agreements, and to intensified cooperation with management. The opportunity for the works councils is that they can expand their influence into areas of utmost importance for the shaping of qualitatively good working conditions; the risk is that closer integration with management will remove them more and more from their real power base, the trade unions. Until now, however, new technology, flexibility and decentralization have not led to a fundamental change in the relations between industry-wide collective bargaining and company-specific participation.

The positions of trade unions and employers' organizations

One of the reasons for the relative stability of the German industrial relations and participation system is that both trade unions and employers' organizations on the whole accept and support the institutions set up and developed since the Second World War. At the same time, the existing institutions constitute a compromise which both parties in principle are critical of.

It is still the objective of the DGB that labour should have parity representation at all levels where its interests are involved so that overall economic planning, the financial decisions of companies and the managerial function will be based on the shared control and power of capital and labour. This objective has only been reached in the *Montanindustrie* where the trade unions see parity on the supervisory boards as the basis for full participation at all levels of company decisions. Conversely, the vast majority of German firms which are not covered by parity representation are regulated in a way that does not satisfy the demands of the trade unions (Leminsky 1986: 150–5). On the other hand, the unions have realized that their concept of full co-determination cannot be implemented even under a Social Democratic government, and consequently their strategy is not to change the system fundamentally, but to develop their own strength and expertise in order to exploit the possibilities inherent in the employee representation on works councils and supervisory boards (Leminsky 1986: 151).

This moderation of goals was particularly influenced by experience gained from the reforms of the co-determination laws in the 1970s. Here the BDA (Bundesvereinigung der Deutschen Arbeitgeberverbände) strongly opposed an extension of the full parity of the *Montanindustrie* to all companies with over 2,000 employees, arguing that parity infringes on the property right guaranteed by the constitution and makes the employers' associations dependent on the opposing side, thus preventing the collective bargaining system from functioning according to its purpose (Federal Minister 1980: 22–33). The pressure from the employers' confederation resulted – as mentioned earlier – in an employee representation which *de facto* does not amount to parity. This was confirmed by the Federal Constitutional Court in its ruling in relation to an appeal lodged by the employers' organizations. Although the court carefully abstained from voicing any opinion on the constitutionality of co-determination based on full parity, the whole political and legal process showed that powerful forces in German society are not willing to accept the participation concept of the trade union movement.

The BDA has never accepted the co-determination law for the *Montanindustrie*. It has refused the companies of this sector affiliation on the grounds that they are not independent of trade union and employee interests, and it is determined to resist the spread of full parity to other sectors of the economy.

As for the Works Constitution Act, the BDA is especially critical towards the provisions obliging the employer to negotiate with the works council in case of alterations in the enterprise. The main argument is that in this way, especially if the conciliation committee has to intervene, important decisions will be delayed with financial losses as a consequence (Thüssing 1986: 165). But, on the whole, both this act and the Co-determination Act of 1976 are accepted by the employers' organizations. Yet, the BDA has made its opposition to any extension of participation rights quite clear: 'The system of participation of workers and their representatives . . . has reached the bounds of what is acceptable and admissible if undertakings are to remain capable of operating' (Thüssing 1986: 168). The fact that participation can also have *positive* consequences for the enterprises may be admitted by individual employers, but has until now not been recognized in the policies of their organizations. The power aspect seems to have overshadowed the other dimensions of employee participation.

Overall, however, there is a high degree of *de facto* consensus between the two peak organizations of the German labour market. This was shown, for example, in 1988 when both the DGB and the BDA, unsuccessfully, opposed an amendment to the Works Constitution Act making it easier for minority unions and unorganized employees to be represented on works councils (Schneider 1989: 392–3).

Conclusion

The German participation system is first and foremost based on two important institutions: the works council and representation on supervisory boards.

The representation of employees and trade unions on the supervisory boards amounts only to full parity in the *Montanindustrie*, but even here the participation has not led to any conceivable changes in the overall priorities of the companies. The representatives of labour have cooperated in taking market-orientated decisions, including the implementation of closures and rationalizations. However, the effects of strong labour representation can be seen in the area of social and personnel policies. Here, strong involvement, coupled with the activities of the labour director, has led to more systematic planning approaches, and to the development of practices which are sensitive towards the social and employment needs of employees.

The works council has increasingly become the most important *locus* for employee participation. The extension of co-decision rights, contained in the 1972 revision of the Works Constitution Act, as well as the tendency towards framework collective agreements, leaving the final solutions to be worked out through works agreements, have contributed to the rising significance of the works council. Behind the changing relations between collective bargaining and works agreements are other factors such as: the spread of new technology, the policies of decentralization and flexibility pursued by employers, and a stronger involvement on the part of trade unions in workplace-related strategies.

The actual functioning of the works councils stretches from non-existence to an extensive involvement in management decisions. In general, the role of the works councils has been relatively reactive and defensive in relation to management policies and decisions. Compared to non-participative management systems, it is an important difference, however, that German managers have to obtain the consent of the works councils in such matters as payment systems, overtime or short-time work, and personnel policies, and to seek their consent before engaging in changes which have consequences for working conditions and job content. The extensive co-decision and consultation rights and the close contact between employer and works council also mean that, once taken, a decision is usually acceptable to the employees; their possible opposition has been anticipated in the decision-making process.

In recent years, there has been a tendency for more offensive and proactive intervention on the part of the works councils in relation to some of the hard-core management questions: the design of work organization and jobs, the implementation of technological change, and the development of the skills of the workforce. New managerial strategies as well as qualitative demands raised by the trade unions have been active in furthering this process. In order to go deeper into pro-active areas of participation the works councils need more than ever the expertise as well as the collective strength of the trade unions.

Finally, there is no doubt that the works council institution has contributed to the low degree of industrial conflict in German society. This is not so much due to the absence of a formal right to strike, but rather to the relatively effective interest representation through participation which is made possible by the works councils.

3

Britain: Participation if the Employer Will

Due to its very limited statutory provisions, the British industrial relations system is often characterized as voluntarist. The legal regulation of industrial relations has mainly taken the form of 'immunities', i.e. court rulings allowing trade unions and their members to engage in certain activities which are in breach of common law. For example, the right to associate in trade unions and the right to strike are not defined as positive rights, but as specific exemptions from common law, which in general understands such actions as impinging on the property rights of the employers (Wedderburn 1991: 44–53).

Although this legal framework has changed historically, in accordance with the political–ideological influences underlying different court rulings, it has in general left to the employers and the trade unions a large scope for defining the patterns of conflict and cooperation in industrial relations. With this background, collective bargaining has been seen and has functioned as the normal way of regulating the employment relationship. Collective agreements are not legally binding, and the right to strike, although constrained by labour legislation passed by the Conservative government during the 1980s, has to a large degree remained unrestricted.

The structure of collective bargaining is relatively complex, with negotiations often taking place at industry (national), district, company and workplace levels (ETUI 1990: 50). While the national trade union confederation, the TUC (Trades Union Congress), has no direct powers to negotiate collective agreements, national agreements for specific industries or trades have traditionally been quite important for the setting of wages and working conditions. From the 1960s, however, a strengthened shop steward movement contributed, often informally, to a decentralization of bargaining to the workplace level. Since the end of the 1970s employers have given priority to negotiations at the company level, thereby diminishing the significance of the workshop level (shop stewards) as well as the national level (national trade unions and employers' associations) (Crouch 1990; Evans 1991). Related to this, employers' organizations as well as trade unions lost ground as far as affiliation is concerned; trade union membership fell from 55 per cent in 1979 (the highest ever) to around 40 per cent in 1990; by 1993 it was down to between 35 and 37 per cent (Gill 1991: 193; Lecher 1994: 176).

Employee participation in Britain to a large extent reflects the characteristics of the industrial relations system in general: legislation and collective agreements at the national level are relatively unimportant, whereas the company level is decisive; the extent of participation as well as its intensity is first and foremost determined by decisions taken within the individual companies.

Historical outline

Except for provisions on safety representatives and disclosure of information to trade unions, there are no legal provisions regulating employee participation in Britain. Participation has largely been and still is a matter left to the voluntarism of the two parties. Historically, neither trade unions nor employers' organizations have shown a great interest in employee participation at the workplace: employers have opposed the restriction of management prerogatives, and unions have feared becoming responsible for company decisions and have preferred the role of an independent actor in collective bargaining. The attempts which have taken place to further the participation of employees have most often been initiated by the government, as a means to improve the social integration of the labour force in critical situations.

The first government initiative came as a response to the militant shop steward movement which grew out of the labour conditions and the politically revolutionary currents during the First World War. In 1917 the Whitley Committee on the Relations of Employers and Employed proposed the setting up of councils composed of employers and union representatives. The councils were to be constituted in each industry, from the workshops to the national level, and to discuss not only wages and working conditions, but also questions related to productivity and management (Pelling 1971: 160). Because of resistance from both left-wing unionists and many employers, the 'Whitley councils' failed to be implemented in most of the private sector, and where they were implemented they soon lost their significance. However, in some of the public services they did become established and remained in operation.

During the Second World War, a rise in shopfloor activities and unofficial strikes again caused disruptions that made it imperative for the government to improve employment relations. National and regional production boards with trade union representation were set up, and they made serious efforts to develop a consultative machinery in the factories (Pelling 1971: 215–16). Yet, these endeavours were so closely linked to the specific war situation that the consultation committees established soon withered away after May 1945.

When the Labour government nationalized a number of industries just after the war, this was not accompanied by any fundamental change in management structures, the predominant view being that a representation of employee interests in the management of the nationalized companies would endanger their efficiency (Coates 1975: 48–51). The nationalization acts contained provisions for the establishment of joint consultation committees – from the national to the workplace level – but there was no mention of co-decision rights (Coates & Topham 1970: 322–7). Although this was in contrast to a strong tendency within the Labour Party which supported the demand for 'workers' control', it was fully in accordance with the official policy of the trade union movement.

The TUC position was stated unambiguously in the report to its congress in 1949: the trade union movement 'should retain its complete independence of the executive and employing authority of a nationalised industry. Only thus can unions exert their power of independent criticism and perform without divided loyalties their primary functions of maintaining and advancing the working conditions of work people' (Edmonds 1977: 4.4).

Only by the 1970s did the Labour Party and the TUC abandon these negative visions of employee participation in managerial decisions. In 1973, a majority of the TUC, as a surprise to many trade unionists as well as employers, came out in favour of trade union representation on the company boards by demanding parity between trade union and owner representatives (Edmonds 1977: 4.17D). The 1973 Labour Party programme also contained demands for trade union representation on company boards as well as demands for legislation that could support the creation of 'joint control committees' in the enterprises (Coates 1975: 213). These demands may have reflected genuine wishes for industrial democracy in its own right, but must also be seen as an integrative response to what was termed 'the challenge from below': the spread of shopfloor militancy, strikes and factory occupations which had taken place in the late 1960s and early 1970s (Knudsen & Sandahl 1974; Wedderburn 1977: 1.9).

After the Labour Party had returned to power in 1974 it set up a committee to consider how to fulfil 'the need for a radical extension of industrial democracy in the control of companies by means of representation on boards of directors' (Benedictus et al. 1977: iv). The result was the Bullock Report which, on the basis of an analysis of the industrial relations 'disorder' in Britain and influenced by Scandinavian and German solutions, opted for a parity representation on company boards for union-appointed shop stewards in companies with more than 2,000 employees. It envisaged a board of directors consisting of an equal number of employee and employer representatives plus a small number of 'neutral' members appointed by the two sides in agreement – a division of seats resembling the one in force in the German *Montanindustrie*.

The stated aims of the Bullock proposal were to provide scope for the growing power and unused capacities of organized labour, to encourage the development of a new partnership between capital and labour in the control of companies, and to improve the efficient operation of the companies (Bullock 1977). It provoked an, at times, heated debate on the principles of industrial democracy in Britain, but legislation based on the proposal failed to be adopted because of the strong opposition to it, and in the end because of the electoral victory of the Conservative Party in 1979.

The Bullock Report was heavily criticized by the Confederation of British Industry (CBI) and other employer organizations (Methven 1977), but also by strong sections of the trade union movement. These trade unions feared being co-opted to management responsibilities, and they were opposed to the loss of independence in collective bargaining which they thought the proposal would entail; they argued that industrial democracy should be promoted through an extension of collective bargaining rather than through parity representation at board level (Taylor 1977).

However, the Labour government succeeded in passing two other pieces of legislation containing provisions for employee participation. First, the Health and Safety at Work Act of 1974 made it possible for trade unions to appoint official safety representatives in the workplace, and mandatory for employers to consult with these and to form a safety committee if so requested by the safety representatives (ETUI 1990: 52). Secondly, the Employment Protection Act of 1975 established that employers are obliged to disclose relevant information on issues such as pay, manpower statistics, production performance, and the financial situation to representatives of those trade unions with which the employer conducts collective bargaining (Hussey & Marsh 1983: 9.16). Roughly speaking, the information to be disclosed is limited to issues which are traditionally subject to collective negotiations. Thus, neither the act nor the related code of practice mentions information in relation to, for instance, technical or organizational changes.

The Conservative government in power since 1979 has been opposed to any kind of legal rights concerning employee participation. The government has considered it important to curb trade union influence and to support the managerial autonomy of employers. In the EC arena, the British government has fiercely resisted different initiatives from the Commission aimed at harmonizing the participation institutions of the member states. In December 1991, this struggle reached a culmination when the summit meeting in Maastricht decided that Britain, instead of continuing to block common labour regulations, in the future should be allowed to be exempted from EC decisions in this field.

At the same time, the British trade union movement seemed to become a more whole-hearted supporter of institutionalized participation rights. At least since 1988, the TUC has unreservedly supported the EC/EU initiatives aimed at introducing a minimum degree of employee participation in all companies operating within the Community (TUC 1988). In general, as British unions have experienced a loss of power at the national level, they have increasingly orientated themselves towards Brussels.

Despite the almost complete lack of any statutory participation rights, British workers have to a considerable extent been able to take part in decisions which traditionally fall under the heading of management prerogatives. The main vehicle for this has been the shop stewards, but in a substantial number of companies more formal bodies for participation, in the form of 'joint consultation committees', have been established.

Shop stewards

Shop stewards were known in the metal industry well before the First World War, their main function originally being the negotiation of piecework rates with the employer. Historically, the spread of the shop steward institution was partly fuelled by the aspirations of the trade unions to establish a foothold inside the enterprises, partly by workers themselves wishing to have local spokesmen for the furthering of their interests. The function of the shop steward is essentially to put forward the grievances and demands of the employees through negotiations and consultations with management. Bargaining with the employer – whether it be in coordination with the union at branch, district or national level, or independently – is the most important method of interest representation, but in many cases bargaining is supplemented by consultation.

In most British companies there are several trade unions present. Shop stewards are usually elected by the members of a specific union in a given workshop or department. In larger enterprises the shop stewards coordinate their activities through a joint shop stewards committee and by electing a senior shop steward or convener. The rules governing the facilities given to stewards, and their rights with regard to paid time off, are in some cases determined by national collective agreements; in others they are fixed at the enterprise level (Clegg 1976: 13–15).

The activities of shop stewards are still to a large extent informal, in the sense that even though their role and scope of action may be prescribed through union rule books and collective agreements, their actual dealings primarily reflect the wishes of their constituency and the customs and practices developed over time in their relation to management. The informality of the shop steward institution has proved to be its strength and its weakness: in periods with a tight labour market such as during the two world wars and in most of the period from 1945 to 1975, the number of shop stewards as well as their influence were able to grow, whereas periods of recession, as for example most of the 1980s, have uncovered the volatile and vulnerable nature of the shop stewards' position (Hyman 1975: 152–3; Gill 1991: 207–9).

By the end of the 1960s shop stewards were an almost universal feature of British industrial relations in the public as well as the private sector. A study of their activities published at that time showed that most shop stewards negotiated over wages, working hours and overtime. In addition, between 20 and 30 per cent said that, as standard practice, they dealt with redundancy, suspensions and dismissals, the manning of machines, the introduction of new machinery and new jobs, and with the distribution, pace and quality of work, and many more said that they did so sometimes (Clegg 1976: 12–13). These were issues rarely covered by formal collective agreements, thus witnessing that shop stewards participated to a considerable degree in management decisions at the operational level. Depending on the power relations and the industrial relations climate in individual companies, the participation could take the form of cooperation as well as confrontation with management.

Although the number of shop stewards kept growing during the 1970s, their power began to decrease from the late 1970s as a result of a combination of the pressure of mass unemployment, and the determination of managers to restrict the activities of stewards. Management sought a higher degree of formalization of the role of shop steward, and insisted on a centralization of bargaining so that issues were settled through formal company-wide negotiations rather than informal negotiations at workshop or plant level (Gill 1991: 209). From the 1980s there is evidence of a gradual reduction of the power of shop stewards. The methods used by management included:

> the enforcement of longstanding procedures which had fallen into disuse, such as the steward having to obtain a supervisor's permission to leave a job on union duties; limiting the number of shopfloor meetings allowed in working time to that specified in the agreement . . . restricting the issues on which management was willing to bargain, communicating directly to employees rather than through shop stewards. (Morris & Wood 1991: 271)

In general, there is no doubt that the period since the end of the 1970s has seen a weakening of the shop stewards' role as workplace negotiators. Whether the intensity of their participation in managerial

decisions has decreased too, is a much more open question. The fragmentation of British industrial relations to the company level makes a
general assessment difficult. While some companies prefer to manage
without the interference of trade unions and shop stewards at all,
others try to develop a more cooperative management style where the
participation of both the employees and their shop stewards is promoted. At least for these companies, a tendency can be observed for
dealing with a number of qualitative issues through participation mechanisms rather than through confrontation and collective agreement.

Joint consultative committees

As already mentioned, joint bodies for consultation were advanced by
the state during the two world wars and within the nationalized industries, but none of these initiatives had a lasting impact on workplace
industrial relations. In the inter-war years, a few of the large companies
in the private sector chose to set up consultation committees, partly as
an alternative to dealing with trade unions and shop stewards. For
example, when the ICI group in 1927 decided to establish works committees in all its plants, shop stewards were not recognized, and the
representatives of the workers on the committees were to be elected by
all employees irrespective of trade union affiliation. In 1947, however,
the company recognized shop stewards and from then on maintained a
dual system of employee representation (Clegg 1976: 187–91).

Most often the initiative to establish a joint consultative committee
is taken by the management which at the same time defines the scope of
its activities; in other cases, an agreement between management and
unions or shop stewards provides the basis for the committee (Poole
1986a: 72). Similarly, there are variations as to how the employee representatives are selected; they may be nominated by the trade unions
and be identical to the shop stewards or, at the other extreme, they may
be chosen through an election among all employees.

While shop steward organizations grew in number as well as importance in the period from the 1940s to the 1960s, joint consultative
committees often ceased to exist or practically fell into disuse (Clegg
1976: 192). But at least since 1975 there seems to have been an increase
in both their number and significance.

Surveys from the first half of the 1980s covering establishments with
at least 25 employees showed that joint consultative committees existed
in a little over 30 per cent of private workplaces and in around 45 per
cent of public workplaces (Daniel & Millward 1984: 129–41; Millward
& Stevens 1986: 138–47). Besides, some of those workplaces without a
committee of their own were represented on higher-level consultative
committees within the company or group of companies they formed

part of. Joint consultative committees were clearly more frequent in establishments recognizing trade unions than in non-union establishments, and larger workplaces were considerably more likely to have committees than smaller ones. In a majority of committees both manual and non-manual workers were represented, but it is noteworthy that in nearly half of the committees employee representation consisted of either manual workers only or non-manual workers only (Millward & Stevens 1986: 143). The most predominant matters to be discussed by the committees were production and employment issues, and participation and consultation arrangements.

A survey conducted in 1990, in which large workplaces were somewhat over-represented, found that 40 per cent of private sector companies had joint consultative committees (Scott 1991: 509). The study showed that the committees met more regularly and covered a wider range of issues than before. According to the managers interviewed, nearly three-quarters of the committees met at least once every two months. The issues discussed ranged from financial results to issues related to productivity, quality improvement, and welfare issues. A further finding of the study was that firms which recognize trade unions for collective bargaining showed a marked tendency to consult on a wider range of issues than non-union firms. Similarly, foreign-owned workplaces had consultation on more issues than British-owned. Finally, the results showed no signs of consultation tending to replace collective negotiations; rather consultation was seen to augment collective bargaining (Scott 1991: 511).

Although there appears to have been an overall growth in consultation arrangements since the 1970s, different case studies have produced contradictory results as to the qualitative changes at play, reflecting a variety of management strategies and probably also different market conditions. The studies indicate that some companies have used the favourable power relations during the recession to dispense with joint consultation and participation, while other categories of firms have intensified consultation, either as a means of reducing the importance of trade unions, or as a supplementary mechanism to already existing arrangements with unions and shop stewards (Crouch 1990: 337; Morris & Wood 1991). Some companies, notably Japanese multinationals, have shown an evident interest in consultation practices, but this does not necessarily lead to the establishment of representative bodies: direct communication to the individual employees, and their involvement through quality circles, workshop meetings etc., are in some cases used as an alternative to consultation committees. One case study indicates that such forms of direct participation have been increasing, sometimes at the expense of indirect forms of participation through shop stewards and consultation committees (Morris & Wood

1991). The study by Scott (1991) found that direct forms of participation (such as quality circles, working parties and team briefings) have increased, but not at the expense of joint consultative committees.

The growth in joint consultative committees must essentially be seen in the context of changing management strategies: by trying to restrict the bargaining scope of shop stewards, and offering consultation procedures as a supplement to collective bargaining, managers want to take issues such as work organization, manning levels etc. out of the relatively conflictual and adversarial negotiation relationship and place them within a more cooperative and peaceful setting. And by building up relations based on trust and cooperation, firms will be better suited to adapt to the insecurity stemming from rapidly changing market conditions and technological innovation. This latter aspect will be elaborated below.

Health and safety committees

An exception to British voluntarism is the 1974 Health and Safety at Work Act and the regulation from 1977 on Safety Representatives and Safety Committees. Before this legislation, health and safety was formally a matter to be handled exclusively by the employers and the Factory Inspectorate. In reality, it was also an issue for collective bargaining, and especially in the larger companies joint management/union health and safety committees had often been established (Glendon & Booth 1982: 405; Vogel 1991: 103).

The legislation on health and safety provides that recognized trade unions may appoint safety representatives from among the employees. Safety representatives are secured time off with pay in order to receive training and to fulfil their functions: to investigate hazards, causes of accidents, and workers' complaints, to carry out inspections and consult with inspectors, and to communicate with the employer. They have no powers to suspend work, but have a right to receive relevant information and to be consulted by the employer on questions related to health and safety.

Consultations of a more general character take place on the health and safety committee which the employer is obliged to establish if requested by the safety representatives. By the early 1980s about 60 per cent of unionized establishments were covered by such committees (Poole 1986a: 77), but at the same time, 16 per cent of private workplaces recognizing trade unions and 43 per cent of those not recognizing unions had no employee representation at all (not even safety representatives) in relation to health and safety matters (Millward & Stevens 1986: 150). Surveys conducted in 1979 and 1987 demonstrated an increase in the number of safety representatives for firms with more than 250 employees; in firms with less than 100 employees, however, a clear decrease could be observed (Vogel 1991: 105)

It is remarkable that the legislation in reality only applies to firms where one or more trade unions are recognized by the employer; non-union companies have no obligation to have safety representatives elected or to form a health and safety committee. This principle was adopted after pressure from the TUC and is in accordance with the traditional British trade union demand that trade unions should enjoy a monopoly in representing employees.

Trade unions have chosen different policies in relation to the appointment of safety representatives. Some have preferred to appoint persons who are already elected as shop stewards, while others have found it important to have different persons so that the mainly participative function of safety supervision could be kept apart from the mainly bargaining function of the shop steward. Both the TUC and some of the individual trade unions have developed training courses for safety representatives.

The legislation on safety representatives and committees has no doubt strengthened the awareness of health and safety matters in the workplace as well as contributed to a higher degree of employee participation in this field. On the other hand, it has not led to the improvements hoped for by the trade union movement (Glendon & Booth 1982; Vogel 1991). This may be due to the relatively limited powers and mainly reactive role assigned to the safety representatives. The legislation does not envisage proactive intervention by the safety representatives in those processes which shape the work environment, i.e. technical development and planning and the design of workplaces, technologies and jobs. Nor is the British trade union movement well equipped to enter into such active forms of participation.

New technology and participation

The introduction of new technology based on computer control and electronics often requires a comprehensive restructuring of work in order to be successful. Such restructuring, involving major changes in job content, skill requirements etc., can only be implemented successfully if the workforce is cooperative and committed to the changes. The British industrial relations tradition has created severe obstacles to cooperative relations between management and workers (Lane 1989: 186). The tradition has been for management to decide unilaterally at strategic and tactical levels, while at the operational level unions and shop stewards have been engaged in 'getting the best out of it' for the employees. This has involved continued bargaining processes and the potential or actual use of industrial conflict as a pressure instrument.

Also, the lack of institutionalized participation rights or guaranteed positions have led unions and shopfloor organizations to rely on their immediate strength here and now, and to stress the adversarial aspects of the relationship with employers. Rather than looking for gains from future developments, they have often focused on the defence of what has been won in the past, thus to some extent acting as a conservative and reactive force in relation to technological and organizational change.

Of course, these characteristics should not be over-estimated; in many firms much more cooperative relations have emerged. Managements introducing new technology have responded in different ways to the relatively conflictual industrial relations setting. Some have accepted the conflictual state of affairs, taken a unilateral decision to introduce new technology, and then bargained with the shop stewards over pay and conditions during and after implementation. The short-comings of this approach are, first, that it fails to mobilize any commitment on the part of the workers in relation to the changes; sec-ondly, that it makes it difficult for management to assess the costs and advantages of the new technology beforehand. Other companies have deliberately attempted to use the process of change to weaken shopfloor organizations and their control over the labour process (Price 1988; Morris & Wood 1991). This approach obviously is equally unlikely to promote the commitment of employees, and the risk of overt or covert conflicts is increased. Finally, a third category of com-panies has consciously aimed to increase participation in order to enhance the control over the process of change and the likelihood that it will be successful.

A study by Price (1988) demonstrated that rather than the existence of a formal technology agreement, the general industrial relations cli-mate in a firm was the most important factor in deciding whether workers obtained influence over the introduction of new technology or not. In firms characterized by cooperative relationships between employer and employees, the introduction of new technology was accompanied by an intensification of both direct and indirect forms of participation; whereas in firms with a markedly conflictual industrial relations profile, management did not invite employees or shop stew-ards to take part in decision-making. In several of the cooperation-orientated firms, employee participation amounted to a proactive involvement in the choice of technology, job design and the formulation of re-training needs. According to the description of one case 'both stewards and management agreed that their ideas and approach to the new systems changed radically as a consequence of these group discussions' (where both employees, stewards and man-agers took part) (Price 1988: 255).

In a survey from 1984 detailed statistical evidence was provided concerning the participation of employees in incidences of relatively comprehensive technological change (Daniel 1987: 112–51). According to the responses of managers, the change was negotiated (co-decided) with shop stewards or other union representatives in only about 6 per cent of cases. The frequency of different forms of consultation (taking place at least once before or during the change) is shown in table 3.1, taken from Daniel (1987: 120).

These figures say nothing about the intensity of the consultations. But its modesty is hinted at by the fact that only 19 per cent of the shop stewards reported that they were consulted both before the introduction of technical change and during its implementation. While the extent of participation was related positively to enterprise size, as could be expected, it may seem surprising that even participation through non-union channels (for example, joint consultative committees or direct discussions with workers) was much more frequent in those establishments which had recognized unions than in non-unionized workplaces. In 44 per cent of the cases there was no consultation at all in the latter type of workplace. Another conspicuous finding was that participation was more likely in cases where the technological change lacked the support of the workers than in cases where they had a positive attitude. Daniel (1987: 125) concludes that 'levels of consultation were remarkably low . . . We found too, that managers tended to consult only when they were required to do so, in response to either trade union structures or initial resistance from workers or their representatives.'

Overall, new technology has undoubtedly been active in extending and intensifying participation arrangements in British firms. But the scepticism of many employers towards involving employees and unions in decision-making has prevented them from using participation as a positive and active means of facilitating and reaping the full potential of technological change. Nor has there been any realization of the

Table 3.1   *Frequency of different forms of consultation during comprehensive technological change*

Form of consultation	%
Shop stewards	39
Full-time union officers	16
Joint consultative committee	17
Special committee	11
Individual workers	58
Meetings with groups of workers	38
No consultation	17

Source: Daniel 1987: 120

goals formulated by the trade union movement around 1980. Here, it was envisaged that technological change should be controlled through joint regulation: 'all change was to be by agreement, full information disclosure should take place, unions should be involved in systems design . . . there should be substantive agreements to protect jobs, reduce working time, provide retraining and strict health safeguards' (Price 1988: 249). Not only have employers in general refused the idea of joint regulation; the unions themselves have also failed to come forward with alternative visions of job design and work organization and other qualitative aspects related to new technology, and most employees have had to adapt to new technology in a relatively passive way. This may be a problem for the trade unions, but certainly also for the employers.

The positions of trade unions and employers' organizations

During the discussions on the Bullock Report in the 1970s the major British employers' organization, the Confederation of British Industry, put forward an alternative proposal. Within a legal framework, a participation agreement should be negotiated in each major company or group of companies, and approved by a ballot among all employees. The state was to provide an instrument for arbitration and ultimately to impose a participation scheme with certain minimum requirements on companies where agreement failed to be reached between the parties (Methven 1977). The proposal reflected the pressures put on employers at that time, and it was not upheld when the political tide shifted with the advent of the right-wing Thatcher government in 1979. British employers have fallen back to their traditional position which is that any provision for employee participation should be left to voluntary decisions within individual companies; in general they are 'both resolutely against any participation at board level and also do not favour greater participation by shop stewards at lower level' (Lane 1989: 242).

The position of the trade union movement has also changed since the Bullock debate. The TUC has abandoned the demand for parity representation on company boards, partly as a consequence of the lack of support for this idea among the trade unions at large, and partly as an adjustment to the harsher political climate since 1979. Like the employers, the TUC has reversed to more traditional viewpoints: an extension of the influence of workers is envisaged first of all through a widening of the agenda for collective bargaining so that crucial investment decisions can also be a matter for collective agreements. At the same time statutory regulations are demanded in order to improve the information, consultation and representation rights of employees and their representatives, but it is stressed that the size and scope of representation will be open to discussion and agreement with the employer at company level (Labour Party 1986).

During the 1980s the TUC protested strongly, but in vain, against the successful endeavours of the British government to block any attempt from the EC Commission to introduce statutory participation rights at Community level; nor did the TUC and the Labour Party succeed in the early 1990s in their opposition to the Conservative government's decision to opt out of the social dimension of the Community.

Conclusion

From a purely formal viewpoint the British industrial relations system has very little to offer concerning employee participation. Only in the field of health and safety are the representatives legally empowered to take part in the decision-making process.

Apart from this, employee participation in Britain is a reflection of the voluntarist character of the system. Whether it exists is mainly dependent upon specific company and workplace conditions such as management style and trade union strength, the most important institutions being shop stewards and joint consultative committees.

Different studies indicate that the influence of the shop stewards reached a peak in the late 1960s and early 1970s and has diminished somewhat since then. Parallel to this there has been an increase in the number of consultative committees and similar bodies, signalling a change from more adversarial relationships to a higher emphasis on mechanisms promoting consensus. Nevertheless, it still seems to be the fear of trouble rather than the chance of success that stimulates employers into accepting the participation of employees in decision-making. There is no strong evidence of employers deliberately using participation in an active way in order to develop human resources and improve productivity. Nor are there any strong signs of unions trying to develop participation in order to intervene proactively in the priorities of companies.

The fundamental weakness of the voluntary British system of participation is, in the absence of any legally guaranteed rights for employees, that both parties are tempted to rely on their immediate position of strength and on opportunistic short-term assessments of possible gains. This makes it difficult to build up those relations of trust which are a prerequisite for genuine participation. Under these circumstances it is understandable that many trade unions cling to collective bargaining as the most effective way to obtain influence, while many employers see unilateral decisions as the most efficient way to manage. The present is a product of the past.

4

Spain: Participation within an Adversarial Setting

The Spanish industrial relations system is essentially a new system based on legislation and agreements adopted during the first ten years after the collapse of the Franco dictatorship in 1975. The Constitution of 1978 explicitly states the right to organize in a trade union, the right to strike, and the right to collective bargaining between representatives of workers and employers. It also obliges the public authorities to promote 'the various forms of participation in the enterprise' (Martín Valverde et al. 1991: 110).

Since the late 1970s, legislation on employee and trade union rights has defined a relatively detailed framework for the relations between employers and employees, one of the characteristic features being a dual system of representation through works councils and trade unions respectively. At the enterprise level elected employee representatives and works councils enjoy a wide range of powers, including the right to conclude collective agreements. Under certain conditions, trade unions can also enter into collective bargaining at enterprise level, their main functions being, however, to negotiate agreements at higher levels, i.e. at the provincial, regional or national level, and to represent the interests of workers in negotiations with the government and other state bodies (Knudsen 1991: 79–96).

Spanish employers are organized in the CEOE (Confederación Española de Organizaciones Empresariales) and have a relatively high affiliation rate. On the union side there are several national organizations, but by far the most important ones are the UGT (Unión General de Trabajadores) and the CC.OO (Comisiones Obreras). Trade union membership is only about 15 per cent, but this is not necessarily indicative of a low trade union influence; 90 per cent of the elected employee representatives in the workplace are union members, and 75 per cent of Spanish employees are covered by a collective agreement (Martín Valverde 1991: 1–26).

The trade union structure is marked by a high degree of centralization and a corresponding weakness at the sectoral or industry level. This, together with a long tradition of workplace bargaining, accounts for the fact that industry-wide collective agreements at national or regional level play a minor role compared to company agreements.

However, agreements above the company level are of considerable significance for many small and medium-sized enterprises (Martín Valverde 1991: 26).

Spanish labour law grants a special status to the 'most representative organizations' and widens the impact of collective bargaining by establishing that agreements concluded by the most representative organizations (usually the CEOE, the UGT and the CC.OO) are binding for all members of a specific bargaining unit, no matter whether they are members of the contracting organizations or not.

On several occasions the government has tried to influence the outcome of collective bargaining (especially the level of wage rises) through tripartite discussions and the conclusion of framework agreements between the main organizations. Nevertheless, the company level remains the important *locus* for the settling of actual wages and working conditions. Thus the Spanish industrial relations system combines a centralist and legalist approach on procedures with decentralized decisions on substantials.

Historical outline

A strongly articulated class antagonism has historically been a predominant feature of Spanish industrial relations, and consequently workers as well as employers have been sceptical of any form of participation in the workplace. Although laws on industrial cooperation and workers' participation in management were passed in the inter-war period, their practical implications remained insignificant (de la Villa 1980: 93).

The victory of Franco's forces in the Civil War from 1936 to 1939 led to the complete repression of overt labour conflict through the banning of trade unions and all kinds of independent trade union activities. As an alternative, a labour charter adopted in 1938 introduced the compulsory membership for both workers and employers of the 'vertical trade unions' (*sindicatos verticales*), i.e. corporatist bodies which were to take part in the administration of the statutory regulation of labour relations and working conditions (Alonso Olea & Rodriguez-Sañudo 1988: 24, 36). Within the framework of the vertical syndicates, a structure of employee representation was erected through syndicate liaisons (*enlaces sindicales*), and from 1947 also through works committees (*jurados de empresa*) (de la Villa 1980: 95).

The proclaimed function of the *enlaces sindicales* was to assist the employer in the management of the enterprise. At first, the worker representatives were simply appointed by the employer, but from 1947 an election procedure was used. The *jurados de empresa* were mixed bodies consisting of representatives for workers, technical staff and the employer and had the function of promoting cooperation between the different categories of personnel, the overall ideological context being the enterprise as a harmonious community.

While the workers in the 1940s and 1950s responded to this forced trade unionism and participation by showing lack of interest and passivity, the situation changed during the 1960s and 1970s. Workers began to exploit the possibilities of interest representation through the *enlaces sindicales* and *jurados de empresa* and also through more independent forms of association such as workers' committees (*comisiones obreras*). These claimed to act within the legal framework and, for example, put up candidates to the elections in the vertical trade unions (ILO 1985: 24–5). The activities of these *de facto* independent workers' associations were met partly by repression, partly by indulgence. At the same time certain aspects of anti-union legislation were slackened, and just before Franco's death, in 1975, a decree spelt out the rights to information and consultation of the representatives in the *jurados* (de la Villa 1980: 97–8).

Thus, what started as the total repression of all types of independent working-class activity, developed into a pattern of formal and informal structures making possible a genuine interest representation. One of the central questions for the trade union movement in the transition period after the Franco regime, then, was to what extent these structures should be maintained or abolished. The *comisiones obreras* which developed into a national trade union confederation (CC.OO) were in favour of a high degree of continuity in the sense that they wanted to base trade unionism on the unitary bodies developed in the workplaces during the struggle against the Franco regime. Contrary to this, the other important trade union confederation in post-Franco Spain, the UGT, opted for the creation of structures that would guarantee a central role to the national trade unions in the workplace. The diverging positions reflected the fact that the CC.OO had its power base among the workers' representatives in the enterprises, while the UGT, having survived the Franco era clandestinely and in exile, lacked a base in the workplace, and was therefore more interested in a strengthening of the rights of the trade union organizations (ILO 1985: 47; Kaiero 1988).

The result was a compromise with certain similarities to the German as well as the Italian industrial relations system: a dual structure of employee representation was established in which formally non-union bodies were to play a predominant role at workplace and company level. Trade union sections were allowed to operate in the workplace, but the activities of trade unions should primarily be directed at the more aggregate levels. Legislation passed in 1980 further defined that the participation of employees in management issues were to take place principally through employee representatives and works councils elected by all employees irrespective of trade union affiliation. Later, certain participation rights were also granted to shop stewards.

However, it would be a misinterpretation to see the Spanish regulations on employee participation as only a result of national traditions and ideas. In the transition period the Spanish political élite was eager to orientate itself towards the European Community. It is hardly a coincidence that, for instance, the information and consultation rights granted to Spanish work councils are very similar to formulations used by the EC Commission in the 1970s in its proposals for worker participation (see chapter 7).

Employee representatives and works councils

The present forms of representation and participation at enterprise level are regulated in a relatively detailed manner through legislation. The most important piece of legislation is the Workers' Statute (Estatuto de los Trabajadores, ET) passed in 1980 and later on amended several times (Rodriguez-Piñero & Ojeda Avilés 1989: 142–237).

The ET establishes the unitary representation system as the predominant principle for employee representation at enterprise level: the representatives are to be elected by all employees irrespective of trade union membership. In workplaces with more than 10 and less than 50 employees, employee representatives (*delegados de personal*) are elected, and this is also the case in workplaces employing between six and 10 persons, if the majority so wishes; in establishments with 50 or more employees, the elected representatives constitute a works council (*comité de empresa*) (ET arts 62 & 63). The powers of the employee representatives of small workplaces and the works councils of the larger ones are identical. For that reason, when the term 'works council' is used in the following it usually refers to both forms of representation.

By the elections of 1986, representatives were elected in 75 per cent of companies eligible under the law (EIRR 1990). As shown in table 4.1, the number of representatives to be elected varies with the size of the workforce (cf. ET arts 62 & 66). For elections to the works councils, employees are divided into two electoral groups, one for skilled and unskilled workers, and one for technical and administrative staff. If agreed upon in collective bargaining, a third group, typically for management staff (excluding top management), can be formed. The different groups of employees are represented proportionally to the number of employees in each group (Martín Valverde et al. 1991: 259–60).

In general terms, the official functions of the unitary bodies (*delegados de personal* and *comités de empresa*) are to realize the 'right to

Table 4.1   *Number of works councillors according to workforce size in Spain*

Size of workforce	No. of works councillors
6–30	1
31–49	3
50–100	5
101–250	9
251–500	13
501–750	17
751–1000	21
1000+	2 extra for every 1000 or fraction of 1000 with 75 as the maximum

participation in the enterprise', a right mentioned in the Spanish constitution of 1978, and to 'defend the interests' of the employees (ET arts 61 & 63). In these respects, the representatives are empowered with a number of rights, such as rights to be informed and consulted. But they are also empowered to negotiate collective agreements and to call strikes – functions which in most industrial relations systems are typically assigned to the trade unions.

The trade unions, however, are not without formal and real influence at enterprise level. They have a right to put up lists of candidates for the works council election (ET art. 69), and, as already mentioned, about 90 per cent of the representatives elected are trade union members. In reality this means that the unitary bodies and the trade unions work closely together. In fact, works councils are increasingly becoming 'a subsystem connected with the unions by a multitude of organizational and functional links, and sometimes, in complete reversal of the path followed in the 1960s and 1970s, they are becoming a mere extension of the trade unions in the workplace' (Martín Valverde 1991: 15).

In the following sections, the participation functions of the works councils will be presented by looking at:

- the rights and powers of the representatives: information rights, consultation rights, co-decision rights and strike rights;
- the obligations of the representatives;
- the facilities and protection granted to representatives;
- the communication between the representatives and the represented;
- the special regulation for officials in the public sector.

The most important source of regulation is the Estatuto de los Trabajadores, but in some cases participation rights and practices are also agreed upon through collective bargaining, especially at enterprise level (Senovilla & de la Torre 1987).

Information rights   The ET (arts 64.1 & 23.4) establishes that the employer has a duty to inform the representatives on the following issues:

- at least quarterly, on the general evolution of the economic sector which the enterprise belongs to, on the production and sales situation of the enterprise, on its production plans and the likely development for employment;
- on the balance, the annual accounts and the annual report, and in the case of the enterprise being a joint-stock company or a cooperative society, those documents that are distributed to the owners;
- on the types of written labour contracts used by the enterprise, and the documents related to the termination of the employment relation;
- at least quarterly, on the statistics on absenteeism and its causes, work accidents and occupational diseases and their consequences, periodic or special studies on the working environment and the prevention mechanisms used;
- on all sanctions imposed for very serious offences;
- on cases where employees are temporarily moved to lower categorized jobs.

As for some of the information provisions, it is not evident whether the information has to be in writing or whether it can be given orally to the works council or to all employees at a general meeting. A labour court decision of 1987 laid down that the employer is not obliged to supply employee representatives with copies of the documents containing key financial information about the situation of the firm (Rodriguez-Sañudo 1988).

In January 1991 the information rights were extended by a law on labour contracts. The law granted employee representatives the right to obtain abstracts of all new written employment contracts (Ley 2/1991). The overall aim of the law was to limit illegal forms of labour relations, for example abusive uses of temporary employment contracts. A regulation of this kind had been demanded by the trade unions, but was strongly resisted by the employers' confederation.

Consultation rights   According to the ET (art. 64) the works council is entitled to put forward opinions on a number of questions related to the management of the enterprise, namely concerning:

- restructuring of the workforce, and total or partial, definitive or temporary closures;
- reductions in working hours, and total or partial removal of installations;

- enterprise plans for vocational training;
- introduction or revision of systems of organization or control of work;
- time studies, the establishment of bonus or incentive systems and job evaluation;
- when the fusion, absorption or the modification of the legal status of the enterprise has consequences for the volume of employment.

The opinion of the works council shall be given within a time limit of 15 days. In these provisions no discussion or negotiation process is envisaged to follow up on the opinions. In reality, however, the opinions may give rise to talks between the employer and the representatives and to formal or informal agreements. In some of the collective agreements the establishment of parity committees is arranged for the continuous discussion of specific issues, such as health and safety, social questions, vocational training, recruitment to vacancies, employment, geographical mobility, studies of new work methods and job evaluation (Senovilla & de la Torre 1987: 130). Though based on the parity principle, these committees usually do not express a state of real co-determination; but most often they act as channels for consultations of a more intensive character than those stipulated by law.

Some collective agreements also include provisions for an extension of the areas where the employer is obliged to inform or to consult with the representatives, but in this respect most agreements only repeat the clauses of the law (Senovilla & de la Torre 1987: 129–33). Two agreements signed in December 1992 – between the peak organizations, and the peak organizations and the government respectively – established a new vocational training system, including the participation of employee representatives in the administration of training schemes at enterprise level (*Employment Observatory* 1993). Further rights to consultation are conceded in ET arts 36 and 51 on:

- the introduction of flexible working time, and
- dismissals due to technological or financial reasons.

In order to go ahead with collective dismissals the employer is required either to obtain the consent of the works council or to get permission from the labour authorities. If the works council refuses to give its consent, the employer has to forward a comprehensive document, including the viewpoints of the employee representatives, to the labour authorities in order to justify the dismissals as necessary for economic or technical reasons. Moreover, the employer must await a positive or negative reply from the authorities. If, on the other hand, the employer gets the consent of the works council, it is for all practical purposes a mere formality to obtain the consent of the labour authorities, and the employer can begin to implement the dismissals 15 days after notification has been given to the authorities (Martín Valverde et al. 1991: 555–6; Vaca 1990: 528–30). As can be seen, the consultation right may here develop into a *de facto* co-decision right.

Co-decision rights   In Spanish labour law there are no expressly stated provisions granting co-decision rights to the works council, except for art. 38.2 of the ET which states that the fixing of a holiday period common for the whole workforce must be based on the consent of both parties.

However, as mentioned above, there are elements of co-decision included in the provisions on collective dismissals. A similar decision-making structure is established in relation to cases of 'substantial modifications of working conditions', i.e. major changes in the length or placement of working hours, shift-work systems, remuneration systems, and work and performance systems (art. 41).

In such cases management may obtain significant advantages from negotiating an agreement with the works council. For, if agreement is reached, the changes do not have to be accepted by the labour authorities; a notification is enough, and the changes may be implemented immediately. In cases of disagreement, on the other hand, the authorities must first be convinced that the proposed changes can be justified on 'technical, organizational or productive' grounds, and, even if they accept the proposal of the employer, their review of the case will delay the implementation of the planned change considerably (Martín Valverde et al. 1991: 515–17; Durán López et al. 1987: 81–4).

Social issues are a further possible area for joint regulation. Art. 64.1.9 of the ET states that the works council shall 'participate, as determined by collective agreement, in the management of social activities established in the enterprise to the benefit of the employees and their relatives'. Collective agreements frequently provide for the setting up of parity committees to deal with social questions: sports and child-care facilities, loans and bursaries to employees etc. These committees usually have an executive character. In some agreements a right to co-decision is also established on issues such as recruitment of new personnel, promotion, and allocation of the better-paid jobs (Senovilla & de la Torre 1987: 130–1).

Finally, it may be mentioned that art. 19.5 of the ET gives employee representatives a unilateral right to decide in situations where they judge that health and safety legislation has been ignored by the employer to the effect that there is an immediate risk of an accident. A decision to stop work in such cases must be supported by 75 per cent of the representatives, or by all of them if the production process in question is continuous. Yet, these provisions only apply to workplaces where there is no health and safety committee; where such a committee exists, it is this, employer-dominated, body which is entitled to stop work.

All in all, one may say that the participation rights granted to Spanish employees are detailed and extensive, but not very intensive. They do not allow employees a strong influence on strategic and tactical matters. Furthermore, it seems that those provisions which do point to a real influence over important issues are not being utilized in an active way by the works councils. Works councils tend to interpret participation rights as a defensive instrument whereas collective bargaining, perhaps backed by the strike weapon, is seen as the more efficient way of gaining influence (Grab & Krüger 1993).

Strike rights   The ET lays down that the works council is empowered to exercise activities of vigilance in relation to the observance of the labour, social security and employment legislation in force, as well as the agreements, conditions and customs and practices in the enterprise in question, and to formulate adequate legal actions towards the employer and the competent courts (art. 64.1.8). Also, the works council is entitled to call strikes if the above-mentioned participation rights are neglected by the employer. The Spanish strike legislation does not forbid strikes on matters concerning the interpretation of collective agreements or matters that are not covered by such an agreement (Alonso Olea & Rodriguez-Sañudo 1988: 144).

Obligations   According to the ET, employee representatives are obliged to cooperate with the management of the enterprise in order to secure the maintenance and growth of productivity (art. 64.1.10). Further, they have a professional secrecy in relation to all types of information they receive in their capacity as representatives (art. 65.1). The scope of professional secrecy is in principle defined by the employer, but can be tried before the labour courts.

The obligation to cooperate in order to promote productivity is in some collective agreements specified through the establishment of a parity committee on productivity. Its purpose is to discuss technical–organizational matters as well as personnel questions such as absenteeism and work performance (Senovilla & de la Torre 1987: 130–4).

It is noteworthy that, in the legislation and usually also in collective agreements, the cooperation function of the representatives is separated from the participation function based on rights to information, consultation and negotiation.

Facilities and protection   Employee representatives are entitled to have adequate office space and notice boards, if the circumstances so permit, in the workplace or enterprise where they function (art. 81). Further they are permitted to have paid time off in order to fulfil their representative functions, the number of hours per month ranging from 15 for each representative in enterprises with up to 100 employees, to 40 in enterprises with over 750 employees; through collective bargaining a pooling of hours can be agreed upon allowing one or more of the representatives to have more time off than the rest (art. 68.e). Extra hours are given for participation in meetings called at the initiative of the employer. In large companies these rules permit one or several works councillors to function as representatives on a full-time basis.

Employee representatives enjoy special protection in relation to dismissals. During the period in office and the following year, a representative cannot be dismissed because of his/her activities as a representative (art. 68.c). If the representative is dismissed and this act is found unfair by the labour court, the representative has a right to reinstatement, but can also choose compensation instead (art. 56.3). This is different from the general provision concerning dismissals where the employer is the one who has the right to choose between reinstatement and compensation (art. 56.1). Finally, in cases of redundancies due to financial or technological reasons the representatives have priority with regard to keeping their jobs (art. 51.9). This is also the case in relation to temporary or permanent transfers ('geographical mobility') (art. 40.5).

Communication between representatives and the represented   The ET establishes that the works council must inform the employees on all matters which may have consequences for labour relations (art. 65.1). Furthermore, it institutionalizes the employee assembly as a forum for communication between employee representatives and the totality of employees (arts 77–80). This assembly, or general meeting, can be summoned by the representatives or 33 per cent of the employees. The employer is obliged, if possible, to make an adequate room available for a meeting every second month, and the representatives for their part are obliged to inform the employer about the time and agenda of the meeting, and of the participation of persons not belonging to the enterprise. The meetings must take place outside normal working hours, unless provisions in the collective agreement decide differently.

The assembly is the most important channel of communication between the representatives and the represented, thus supplementing the representative system with a forum for direct democracy. Although the function of the assembly is mainly consultative, it is empowered to vote on agreements covering the whole workplace or enterprise (art. 80), and to recall representatives within the normal election period of four years (Martín Valverde et al. 1991: 275–8).

Officials in the public administration   This category of employees, whose labour relations are not determined through collective bargaining but by direct state regulation, is excluded from the participation provisions of the Estatuto de los Trabajadores. In 1987, however, a law was passed which extended the unitary representation system to officials employed in the public administration. The law by and large provided the representatives of the officials with rights and obligations similar to those enjoyed by the works council in relation to taking part in management issues (Martín Valverde et al. 1991: 263).

Other channels for participation

Shop stewards   Spanish labour law not only regulates the election and activities of employee representatives and works councils elected by all employees, but also contains provisions for the election of trade union shop stewards (*delegados sindicales*). This right is limited to enterprises with more than 250 employees and to trade unions which are present in the works council. If, further, the trade unions in question have obtained more than 10 per cent of the votes in the works council election and the enterprise has more than 750 employees, they are entitled to more than one shop steward (with a maximum of four for each union). The Act on Trade Union Freedom gives the trade union shop stewards almost the same information and consultation rights, and the same protection from dismissal, as enjoyed by the unitary representatives. It also allows them to take part in works council meetings without the right of voting. In practice, the shop stewards are often elected as members of the works council (Martín Valverde et al. 1991: 268–70).

As far as participation rights are concerned, the existence of trade union shop stewards does not add anything new to the content of employee participation. To a great extent the shop stewards share the participation rights of the unitary representatives, but their negotiating powers are weaker as they are normally only entitled to act on behalf of the members of their own union. On the other hand, from the perspective of specific groups of workers, the shop stewards may contribute to an intensification of actual participation activities.

Health and safety committees   A specific type of participation takes place through the health and safety committees created on the basis of a decree from 1971 (Rodriguez-Piñero & Ojeda Avilés 1989: 164–5). Such a committee must be established in enterprises and workplaces with more than 100 employees, and in smaller workplaces with particularly dangerous activities. The committee is composed of a chairman appointed by the employer, three other persons with management positions in relation to health and safety, a secretary appointed by the employer from among the administrative staff, and 3–5 persons, depending on the size of the workforce, chosen by the works council. This piece of legislation from the Franco era secures the hegemony of the employer in the health and safety committee. This is one of the reasons why it lacks popularity among the trade unions and why many collective agreements include additional provisions regarding health and safety activities (Senovilla & de la Torre 1987: 131; CC.OO 1989: 18, 21).

In enterprises without a health and safety committee, the power to control conditions in this area is placed in the hands of the works council (ET, art. 19.3). In the early 1990s negotiations took place between the chief labour market organizations and the government in order to establish new forms of regulations in the health and safety area. To a certain degree these negotiations were influenced by the 1989 EC 'framework directive' on health and safety (see chapter 7).

Trade union participation in state-owned enterprises   In 1986 an agreement was signed by the UGT and the government about trade union participation in state-owned enterprises (García Murcia 1986). The agreement determined that in such enterprises with more than 1,000 employees the trade unions could take part in management, either through a (minority) representation at board level (*consejo de administración*) or through the creation of a parity committee for information and control (*comisione de información y seguimiento*).

The agreement constituted a framework for participation which would only become effective when codified and specified in the collective agreements of the enterprises. Participation could take place on the level of the single enterprise or on the level of the enterprise group, the state-owned enterprises being divided into four groups. On the latter level, only participation through a parity committee was possible as no common management boards exist. These rights were only conferred on the most representative unions: i.e. in the single enterprises, trade unions which had obtained at least 25 per cent of the seats on the works council; and in the groups of enterprises, only those unions which had at least 10 per cent of the works council seats in the totality of state-owned enterprises.

A study of the follow-up of the agreement in collective bargaining showed that agreements at the enterprise group level had specified the number of members, the functions etc. to be given to the parity committees, whereas there were few provisions in the enterprise agreements as to the participation of trade union representatives on the management boards. At the same time, it was found that a few enterprises in the *private* sector seemed to have been influenced by the framework agreement and had accepted the presence of trade union representatives on the company board (García Murcia 1990).

The agreement on public enterprises is interesting because of its departure from the model of participation through bodies of a unitary character which so far has been predominant in the Spanish industrial relations system. The UGT in particular was pressing for an extension of the agreement to the private sector (Saracibar 1986). However, instead of spreading into other sectors, the agreement failed to be renewed when the relationship between the UGT and the socialist government became more one of conflict from the late 1980s.

New technology and participation

The turbulent effects of new technology on working conditions and employment and the desirability of greater employee participation in relation to the introduction of new technology have also been important discussion themes in Spain (Monero Pérez & Moreno Vida 1987). The discussions, however, have not led to any changes in labour legislation or to specific agreements between trade unions and employer organizations at national level. To a certain extent, the provisions mentioned earlier concerning 'substantial modifications of working conditions' and 'technological redundancies', empower employee representatives to take part in decisions connected to the implementation of new technology, but there are no provisions covering the issue of new technology as such.

In some collective agreements at enterprise level, especially in sectors strongly affected by technological change, there are provisions for the creation of parity committees whose aim it is to discuss and follow the introduction of new technology, and to negotiate over such questions as the loss of jobs, the health and safety consequences, changes in job content, and vocational training (Pérez Pérez 1987). The UGT and the CC.OO have demanded negotiation rights and a greater degree of control during the different stages of the introduction of new technology (CC.OO 1989).

In some of the large companies, project groups, including not only engineers but also different categories of workers, have been established in connection with the introduction of new technology (Castillo 1992). Other forms of direct involvement by employees, partly motivated by technological challenges, include quality circles, work teams and task groups functioning in relation to total quality management. While the 1980s saw a considerable growth in various forms of direct participation, the economic recession of the early 1990s seemed to lead to a stagnation. According to Miguélez (1993), works councils are usually not drawn into the decision-making process when forms of direct participation are introduced. At the same time, the reactions of the works councils to management initiatives on this issue have been rather passive (Castillo 1992: 22).

The positions of trade unions and employers' organizations

In 1989 the two trade union confederations, the CC.OO and the UGT, concluded an agreement, *propuesta sindical prioritaria*, defining those trade union demands which were to have priority in the coming years in collective bargaining as well as in negotiations with the government. Among the 20 listed areas where improvements were demanded, two are especially relevant in relation to participation at enterprise level.

First, trade unions demand a general extension of participation rights in enterprises. They propose a change in the law on limited companies in order to establish a clear distinction between the functions of direction and the functions of supervision and control. They demand an equal representation on bodies for supervision and control and a right to participation on management boards (*consejos de administración*). Through collective bargaining, they wish to have the present information, consultation and negotiation rights recognized as 'real powers'; to strengthen negotiations and collective agreements on issues such as working conditions, functional and geographical mobility, work organization, and industrial plans; to obtain a right for trade unions to negotiate before and during the introduction of new technology, especially in relation to employment, working conditions, occupational health, vocational training, and the establishment of control committees (CC.OO 1989: 21). While the demands emphasize trade union co-determination at board level and more participation through collective bargaining, it is remarkable that there are no precise demands for stronger co-decision rights for the works councils.

Secondly, the trade unions propose a revision of the law on health and safety, demanding the establishment of parity committees in all workplaces with more than 50 employees, and the election of a health and safety representative in small enterprises. Also, they want trade unions to have the right to appoint district representatives with the aim of improving working conditions in small and medium-sized enterprises. At the same time, they want the law to establish a broad definition of health and safety matters so that they include the total work environment, i.e. all questions concerning working conditions, work organizations, shift-work, and work methods. The law should also contain an extension of information and consultation rights related to occupational risks, prevention service, and the introduction of new technology. Finally, a consultation right is demanded in relation to investments or production modifications with possible consequences for the environment (CC.OO 1989: 20–1).

While these demands relate to the Spanish industrial relations situation, it is also evident that they are to a large extent inspired by Scandinavian and German standards. They are an example of an increasing Europeanization of trade union policies.

On the employer side, there are no wishes for an extension of general and legally binding participation procedures. The position of the employers' confederation, the CEOE, is that the forms and scope of any additional employee participation must be settled through management decisions at enterprise level or through collective bargaining.

So, at least potentially, participation is a conflict issue between the two parties.

Conclusion

Employee participation in Spain is first and foremost situated in the unitary representation system: employee representatives and works councils. These have comprehensive statutory rights concerning information and consultation. In respect of collective dismissals and substantial changes in working conditions, the consultation rights provide a certain scope for actual co-decision, inasmuch as the acceptance of such changes by the labour authorities is considerably easier to obtain for the employer if an agreement has been reached with the works council. Apart from this, co-decision is only envisaged on issues of minor importance. Co-decision rights, whether based on legislation or collective bargaining, remains the exception rather than the rule.

Several observers of the participation system in Spain have termed it 'collaborationist' with reference to the lack of real power of employees in management decisions in general, and, in particular, to the earlier mentioned obligation of the employee representatives to cooperate with the employer in order to improve productivity (Senovilla & de la Torre 1987: 134–5). This interpretation must be seen against the background of the Spanish tradition of class conflict as a predominant feature of industrial relations, and the associated scepticism towards cooperative structures in enterprises. Yet, compared to other national systems in Europe, the collaborationist elements of the Spanish system are relatively weak. What is conspicuous is rather the detailed and legally guaranteed rights and their character as a 'genuine legal counter-power' (Sobrera 1985: 139) to management prerogatives – a counter-power that may be used in cooperation as well as in conflict with the interests of the employer.

The obligation to cooperate is not supported by specific means to stimulate cooperation, and the participation rights for their part are mainly interpreted as a defence of employee interests *vis-à-vis* management. This is underlined by the fact that they may legally be backed up by strike action. The participation of Spanish employees, then, has an overwhelmingly defensive and reactive character: the employee representatives have powers to react against changes already planned by the employer, but there are few channels and only weak traditions for a proactive part in the development of the enterprise. With regard to possible future development, it can be observed that trade union demands reflect an ambition to strengthen the defensive rights at the same time as more offensive and proactive channels of participation are wanted.

Practically as well as ideologically, Spain has a long tradition of adversarial relations between employers and employees. Until now, the participatory structures established since 1980 have done little to change this tradition. Participation has been interpreted as a resource for employee representatives alongside bargaining and conflict rights within an essentially adversarial setting. And employers, in general, have not actively attempted to turn the works councils into constructive cooperation partners. Because of this, participation has remained relatively insignificant as a mode of regulation.

5

Denmark: Participation as Cooperation

In the Danish industrial relations system legal regulations are scarce. Since the historic September agreement of 1899, when a long and bitter conflict ended by the parties recognizing each other as legitimate bargaining agents, collective agreements have constituted the main instrument for regulating labour relations in Denmark. In the absence of detailed statutory regulation, the rules governing industrial relations are to a large extent worked out through negotiations and central agreements between the two parties or by tri-partite bodies operating within a legislative framework (MISEP 1992).

The main industrial relations parties at central level are Dansk Arbejdsgiverforening (DA) on the employer side and Landsorganisationen i Danmark (LO) on the trade union side. Salaried employees, as well as employees with professional qualifications, have their own trade union confederations. Of the three main organizations, the LO is the only one to have formal ties to a political party, namely the Social Democratic Party. However, as the divisions between the confederations follow professional rather than ideological lines, and as the importance of trade unions not belonging to these three organizations is negligible, the unions in reality constitute a unity movement, with the LO playing the leading role.

Collective agreements are usually sector or trade specific, but highly coordinated by the peak organizations on the one side, and with the possibility of being supplemented by company agreements on the other; they run for two years and are covered by a peace obligation. Lately, decentralization has taken place in the sense that collective bargaining at the sector and company level has gained in importance whereas the role of the peak organizations has declined (Due et al. 1993).

State regulation has largely been confined to providing framework institutions (labour court, conciliation board, labour market boards etc.) conducive to the procedures and goals agreed between the two parties. However, as there are no provisions for a binding arbitration in relation to collective bargaining, the state has intervened several times by dictating the terms of an agreement while referring to vital 'social' or 'national' interests being threatened (Lind 1991).

At enterprise level, shop stewards (*tillidsrepræsentanter*), elected by the members of the trade unions present, constitute the most important channel for the representation of employee interests. Shop stewards are also often the main actors in the more specific participatory institutions: the cooperation committees (*samarbejdsudvalg*), the representation on company boards, and the safety committees (*sikkerhedsudvalg*).

The shop stewards belong to a trade union movement which has a strong organizational apparatus and organizes close to 90 per cent of all wage-earners (Andersen 1993: 63). As will be shown in more detail below, Danish workplace participation, formally as well as in reality, builds on the principle of trade union representation.

Historical outline

The representation through shop stewards which now exists in all sectors of the Danish labour market was first developed in the metal industry where the functions of the shop stewards were recognized by collective agreement as early as 1900. Already in these first rules it was stated that, apart from being the spokesman of the workers in relation to grievances and demands towards the employer, the shop steward has a duty to 'do his best in order to maintain and further a good and smooth cooperation in the shop' (Christensen et al. 1974: 29).

This obligation to cooperate has since become a standard formulation in the rules for shop stewards laid down in the sectoral collective agreements. However, it has never been accompanied by positive rights in relation to employee participation in management decisions. Rather, the obligation to cooperate has functioned as a device to strengthen the peace obligation at workplace level by underlining the responsibility of the stewards in relation to norms defined by collective bargaining and legal regulation.

In the wake of the First World War participation was put on the agenda by the labour movement. Inspired by developments in other countries, notably Germany and Britain, the Social Democratic Minister of Social Affairs in 1924 put forward a proposal to establish works councils in private sector firms with more than 10 employees (Sveistrup 1926: 14–15). Opposition from the right-wing parties, however, prevented adoption of the proposal. On the collective bargaining arena, demands for participation also met with limited success, the only significant result being the workshop meetings agreed upon for the metal industry from 1926. The agreement gave the shop stewards a right to meet with the employer once a month to discuss 'workshop technical issues' (Svane 1965: 103–4).

The demand for works councils was raised again after the Second World War. This time there seemed to be a parliamentary majority in favour of the establishment of such bodies, the debate being influenced by the production committees established in Norway and Sweden at that time. Yet, parliament abstained from legislating when the LO and the DA agreed upon their own formula in order to 'keep the law out'. The result was eventually a national collective agreement on coopera-tion committees (*samarbejdsudvalg*) reached between the two parties in 1947 (Kocik & Grünbaum 1948: 223–5; Lund 1991). In the agreement the employers' federation conceded certain information and consulta-tion rights to the representatives of the workers at workplace and company level, and agreed to a procedure for joint meetings in the cooperation committees.

Since 1947 the cooperation agreement has been renegotiated several times at the initiative of the trade union side; the latest version dates from 1986. In 1981 the LO succeeded in obtaining a technology agree-ment specifying certain participation rights in relation to the introduction of new technology. This agreement was later integrated into the 1986 cooperation agreement. From the beginning of the 1970s cooperation committees were also introduced in the public sector.

Further participation rights were granted through legislation. A change in company law in 1973 enabled employees to elect two mem-bers of the company board; in 1980 the representation was extended to one-third of the board members, two members being the minimum. A new law on health and safety in 1975 led to the establishment of safety groups and safety committees (*sikkerhedsudvalg*) consisting of both employee and management representatives.

The driving force behind the progressive development of institutions for employee participation in the post-war period has been the trade union movement. At the same time it has been of importance that the parliamentary majority for most of the period has consisted of left and centre political parties with relatively favourable attitudes to work-place participation. This has put pressure on the employers' organizations, giving them the option of reaching an agreement directly with the trade unions, or alternatively risking the adoption of legislative measures which would put restrictions on management prerogatives (Lund 1991). The first cooperation agreement from 1947 as well as the 1981 technology agreement were born out of such pressure. On the other hand, both in relation to the collectively agreed and the statutory forms of regulation, the employers have succeeded in avoiding more radical modifications of managerial prerogatives. Seen from this per-spective, the employers are the ones who have been favoured by the parliamentary balance of power because the more far-reaching reform issues, put forward by the socialist parties, have usually been opposed by the centre as well as the right.

It is notable, also, that the most penetrating changes have taken place in periods characterized by low unemployment and intensified rank-and-file activities among workers. While the first cooperation agreement was a consequence of labour's militant position immediately after the Second World War, its renewal in 1970 and the laws of 1973 (representation on company boards) and 1975 (health and safety committees) reflected a growing dissatisfaction with working conditions and authority relations expressed in the late 1960s and early 1970s, especially by the younger generation. The compromises reached between capital and labour and their political representatives during these two phases produced institutional solutions which by now appear to be a well-consolidated part of industrial relations in Denmark.

Cooperation committees: the provisions

According to the Cooperation Agreement (*samarbejdsaftalen*) between the Danish employers' federation (DA) and the trade union confederation (LO), cooperation between employer and employees shall be pursued in all enterprises. In establishments with 35 or more employees a cooperation committee must be established on the request of one of the parties (arts 1 & 4, quoted from Dansk Magisterforening 1991: 391–8). It is stressed that cooperation shall take place at 'all levels of the enterprise' and involve as many employees as possible in the daily organization of activities (art. 1).

The cooperation committee is composed of an equal number of representatives of the employer and the employees. While the management group is appointed by the employer, the representatives of blue- and white-collar workers are selected by and among the shop stewards. If the number of seats exceeds the number of shop stewards, the additional representatives are elected among the rest of the employees (art. 4). The number of committee members in relation to workforce size is shown in table 5.1.

The election period for both groups is two years, and the committee is

Table 5.1   *The composition of cooperation committees in Denmark*

Size of workforce	Employee representatives	Management representatives
35–50	2	2
51–100	3	3
101–200	4	4
201–500	5	5
500+	6	6
1000+	Additional members if agreed upon	

expected to have six ordinary meetings per year. The chairman of the committee is always a 'responsible manager', while the vice-chairman is an employee representative. The importance of the shop steward institution is underlined by the provision that in enterprises with a joint shop steward (*fællestillidsmand*) this person is automatically the vice-chairman of the committee (art. 3). For groups of enterprises, it is recommended that a group committee (*koncernudvalg*) is established, consisting of representatives from the individual cooperation committees and dealing with issues of common interest for the whole group (art. 4).

The main functions of the cooperation committee are defined as to:

- follow and develop the daily cooperation and to involve as many as possible in this activity;
- provide and maintain good and smooth working and employment conditions to increase the well-being and job security of the employees;
- enhance the employees' understanding of the situation of the enterprise regarding its running, financial situation and competitiveness (art. 3).

The committees are not allowed to treat issues which are settled through collective bargaining or local wage agreements. This means that the activities of the shop stewards are divided – also institutionally – into the handling of individual grievances and collective bargaining issues, on the one hand, and cooperation or participation issues on the other.

Information rights   The Cooperation Agreement spells out that, in general, the employers of *all* enterprises are obliged to inform their employees 'at an early time so that viewpoints, ideas and proposals from the employees can be part of the basis for decisions' (art. 2). As for the content of the information, the only factor mentioned explicitly is that management shall give its 'assessment of the consequences of planned changes'. In enterprises with a cooperation committee, the obligation to inform is more specific: according to art. 2, management must inform the employee representatives continuously on:

- the financial situation and future perspectives in relation to the market situation and production conditions of the firm;
- employment conditions;
- larger changes and restructuring, among other things the use of new technology in production and administration.

Information must also be given on the structure and functioning of productivity-related payment systems (art. 3). Further, the cooperation committee itself is obliged to keep all employees informed of its work.

Consultation rights   The cooperation committee is first and fore-most a body for consultations between the two parties. The committee has to be involved in decisions concerning the following issues (art. 3):

- principles for working and social conditions and principles for per-sonnel policy;
- principles for training and retraining of employees in relation to new technology;
- principles for the collection and use of personal data;
- guidelines for the organization of production and work and the implementation of larger changes in the enterprise;
- assessment of the technical, financial, personnel, training and envi-ronmental consequences of technological change, when the change has a 'substantial extent'.

It is also mandatory for management to discuss major lay-offs and changes in ownership. The clauses on these issues implement legal acts from 1977 and 1979 resulting from two EC directives (Lund 1991).

Again, in relation to consultations, it is stated that management must involve the cooperation committee at an early stage in the deci-sion-making process, so that viewpoints and proposals from the employees can be taken into account. In the agreement it is envisaged that the consultations on the committee shall lead to agreement between the parties. Both parties are obliged to aim at agreement on the issues discussed and to carry out in practice what has been agreed. Agreements take the form of principles or guidelines covering the issues mentioned above (notably personnel policy, training, and changes in technology and work organization). Each of the parties can, with two months' notice, terminate an agreement, and demand negotiations on new principles.

Co-decision rights?   Although the Cooperation Agreement uses the term co-determination (*medbestemmelse*) in relation to agreements on principles, the employee representatives do not enjoy a right to co-determination or co-decision in the proper sense. There is no procedure for arbitration or conciliation by a third party in cases where the two parties disagree on *substantials*. Only where employers fail to follow the *procedures* of the Cooperation Agreement, i.e. where they fail to inform and negotiate on the specified issues and to seek agreement, can employee representatives take a case to arbitration (art. 6). But in cases where agreement fails to be reached because of substantial differences in the viewpoints of the parties, management is entitled to decide uni-laterally (Nielsen 1987: 116, 119).

Peace obligation   Neither the employee representatives on the cooperation committee, nor the trade unions to which they are affiliated, have the right to call strikes in response to conflicts that may arise from the negotiations on the cooperation committee. According to Danish labour law, there is a peace obligation in relation to questions which traditionally and through jurisprudence have been defined as falling within the employer's right to manage (Nielsen 1987: 76). As those issues which enter the agenda of the cooperation committee are understood as management issues – open to employee participation but nevertheless issues where the employer has the final right to manage – employees have no formal right to influence the issues through industrial action.

Conflicts related to the application and interpretation of the Cooperation Agreement may be solved through the mediation or conciliation of the Cooperation Board. This is a body with equal representation, established by the two peak labour market organizations (arts 5 & 6).

Obligations towards the employer   The employee representatives of the cooperation committee are obliged to observe professional secrecy in relation to matters which are presented as confidential. Further, they must inform the committee on 'conditions at the workplace which are of importance to the climate of cooperation' (art. 2). Like the employer, they are obliged to aim at reaching agreement.

Facilities and protection   The costs related to the activities of the cooperation committee are paid by the employer. Employee representatives receive their normal pay for the time used for meetings on the committee, but are not entitled to further paid time off (art. 3). In general, there are no provisions for paid time off for exercising the function of shop steward, except for activities carried out at the initiative of the employer. However, some enterprises, especially large ones, have consented to releasing the shop steward from ordinary work without loss of pay (Nielsen 1987: 99).

In case of dismissal, employee representatives who are not shop stewards have a right to six weeks' notice above the notice granted by collective agreement. For others, i.e. the great majority, the conditions negotiated for shop stewards apply. These vary from one collective agreement to the other, but the collective agreements usually grant a longer notice for shop stewards, and in cases of redundancies the shop stewards are the last ones to be dismissed within a given skill group. A dismissal cannot enter into force before the shop steward's trade union has had the opportunity to try the dismissal before an arbitration court. A dismissal found unfair will oblige the employer to pay out compensation, or, rarely practised, to reinstate the shop steward in question (Nielsen 1987: 100–4).

Communication between representatives and employees   While the Cooperation Agreement provides for the dissemination of information to employees on the activities of the cooperation committee, no specific structures are envisaged for the communication the other way, from employees to representatives. In practice, the communication is based on informal procedures and meetings in the workplace units of the trade unions (*klubber*). There are no provisions for employee or works meetings paid by the employer. Nevertheless, such meetings do take place regularly in most of the major enterprises (IP Dansk Institut 1991: 28).

Cooperation agreements for the public sector   Since the beginning of the 1970s, employees in the public sector have also been covered by regulations on participation, first in the form of government circulars, later through collective agreements. In 1981 a technology agreement was negotiated for the state sector, and in 1984 a similar agreement was reached for local government employees. In 1991 new cooperation agreements, which incorporated the former technology agreements, entered into force for the state sector as well as the local government sector (Dansk Magisterforening 1991: 89–95).

The cooperation committees for public sector workplaces are modelled on the ones developed in the private sector, the most important differences being that the public sector agreements:

- put 25 employees as the threshold for establishing a cooperation committee (against 35 in the private sector);
- contain more detailed information and consultation rights in relation to the introduction of new technology, for example by providing for the participation of employee representatives in project groups preparing technological changes;
- entitle employee representatives to demand the establishment of a special technology committee (in the private sector agreement between the parties is needed). (Neergaard 1990: 152)

The public sector agreements thus put employee representatives in a slightly stronger position than is the case in the private sector.

Employee participation in the public sector reaches its highest level in the universities. Since 1970 a special law regulating the management of universities has provided for the direct election of managers and governing bodies at all levels, giving different shares of votes to academic staff, technical and office staff, and students respectively. A revision of the law in 1992 reduced the influence of technical and office staff and students, and gave the elected managers stronger powers *vis-à-vis* the collective bodies (Lov om universiteter m. fl. 1992).

The cooperation committees in practice

In general, the Danish cooperation committees have shown difficulties in living up to the functions assigned to them, but the overall trend has been an increase in their significance. A study undertaken in the late 1950s showed that only around one-third of manufacturing firms had established committees, and only half of these could be characterized as effective according to statements from managers as well as employee representatives (Lund 1991: 178). At the same time, it was noted that the central Cooperation Board had failed to fulfil its functions as a stimulator. A renewal of the agreement in 1964 seems to have blown more life into the committees, for in 1968 it was reported that two-thirds of manufacturing firms with more than 50 workers had established a cooperation committee. Behind the growth was a change in attitudes among employers' organizations, influenced by the full employment situation which made it more difficult to maintain a stable workforce. Also, the strengthening of the Cooperation Board, by the establishment of a secretariat with resources for giving support and advice to individual cooperation committees, was a factor promoting the activities of the committees.

From the end of the 1970s, questions relating to the introduction of new technology became an important issue in Danish industrial relations, undoubtedly contributing to a growth in the extension and activities of cooperation committees. While there were about 900 registered committees in the private sector by the mid-1970s, the number grew to 1,539 in 1990, covering 85 per cent of eligible firms (Samarbejdsnævnet 1991: 20; Lund 1991: 180). A part of this increase was due to the lowering of the threshold in 1986 for establishing cooperation committees: from 50 to 35 employees.

There are no recent investigations on the qualitative practice of the cooperation committees. A study published in 1991 on human resource management in firms with at least 100 employees, showed that only 29 per cent of the enterprises informed the workers systematically about the strategy of the firm, while information on financial matters was given systematically in 54 per cent of firms (IP Dansk Institut 1991: 28). This indicates that the information provisions of the Cooperation Agreement are not being complied with in a great number of companies. One must suspect that consultation and negotiation practices are even less widespread. Press reports on companies violating their obligations to inform and consult are certainly not unusual. On the other hand, there is evidence to suggest that in some firms the cooperation committees are taking an active part in defining management policies on such issues as personnel policy, training, and technical and work organizational changes (Lorentzen 1990; Samarbejdsnævnet 1991). The general impression is, however, that the role of employee representatives is relatively defensive and reactive, the predominant function of the cooperation committee being that of furthering the knowledge, understanding and acceptance of management initiatives among employees, thereby facilitating processes of change and solving potential issues of conflict.

The limited success of the cooperation committees as an instrument for employee participation must be seen in the light of its fragile power base, squeezed as it is between management prerogatives on the one side and collective bargaining on the other. Given the lack of real powers of the cooperation committee, workers have tended to see this body as of minor importance compared to the more traditional channels for interest representation, collective bargaining and the shop steward institution. Employers, for their part, have had no compelling reasons for using the cooperation committee as long as they could further their goals effectively through the ordinary management hierarchy, perhaps combined with meetings with the shop stewards. But tendencies at play since the 1980s – such as the search for flexibility, advanced technical equipment, just-in-time production, and rapid changes in product markets – have led trade unions as well as employers to stress the need for increased participation and cooperation. Although employers often prefer direct, shopfloor-level participation, the search for a closer integration of employees can also lead to a strengthening of the cooperation committees. A development programme launched by the Cooperation Board in 1989 (called 'the club of good examples') was just such an attempt to promote direct forms of participation in coordination with the indirect participation exercised through the cooperation committees (Samarbejdsnævnet 1991).

Representation on company boards

The representation of employees on company boards dates back to one of the rare periods where there was a left-wing majority in the Danish parliament. It was introduced in 1973 as an amendment to existing company legislation and was influenced by expected EC regulations in this area. For this reason, the right-wing political parties and the DA also supported the initiative. Initially, employees were given two seats on the supervisory board (*bestyrelse*) of public limited companies, but since 1980 they have been entitled to elect one-third, and at least two, of the company board members in companies with 35 or more employees; as the board must have at least three members who are elected by the owners, the employee representatives always constitute a minority (Kolvenbach & Hanau 1987/94: Denmark).

Employee representatives are elected among all employees, including lower- and middle-level managers. They serve for four years and have the same rights and duties as other board members, including a secrecy obligation. The board is obliged to inform employees of its activities (Nielsen 1987: 122–3; Lund 1991).

Disagreements between employee and owner representatives on the board are infrequent. A study from 1992 showed that 80 per cent of employee representatives were satisfied with the information they get and the influence they have. Yet, at the same time, about 40 per cent agreed with the statement that power is concentrated in the hands of the president of the board or other 'strong persons'. One-third found that the secrecy obligation prevented them from informing colleagues on essential issues (Alhøj 1992: 6–7). The right to be represented on the supervisory board is only triggered if an initial election shows that at least half of the employees is in favour of it; in a majority of, mainly small, companies, the employees have abstained from using their right to be represented.

The provisions for representation of employees on company boards do not seem to have had any significant repercussions for management practices. Their main effect has undoubtedly been to contribute to an increased knowledge and understanding of management goals and strategies among employees. Neither has the fact that this institution is based on the unitary representation principle caused any noticeable problems for the trade unions.

Health and safety committees

According to the Work Environment Act of 1975, enterprises with 10 or more employees must establish a safety group, consisting of a supervisor and a safety representative elected among the employees. In larger establishments, safety groups must also be formed in individual departments.

In enterprises with more than 20 employees the safety groups must be supplemented by a safety committee (*sikkerhedsudvalg*). In small firms the committee will be identical to one or two safety groups plus the employer or another responsible manager. In medium-sized enterprises the safety committee will typically consist of a chairman representing management and an equal number of supervisors and safety representatives elected from the safety groups. In large enterprises, finally, several safety committees, coordinated by a central committee, can be established (Burg et al. 1982: 13–15).

Safety representatives are elected for a period of two years, and in accordance with the collectively agreed rules for the election of shop stewards. They have the same protection against dismissal as shop stewards, and are entitled to have time off paid by the employer for their activities and for training.

The main function of the safety group is to monitor the health and safety aspects of the work situation; it is empowered to stop work in cases of immediate danger. The safety committee has as its primary goal to plan and coordinate health and safety activities, and to give advice to the management of the establishment. It is explicitly stated that the committee 'shall take part in the planning of the enterprise'. Ideally, this means that the committee must be involved in the planning of work processes and methods, in projects for extending or restructuring the plant, in the introduction and change of machines and other technical devices, and in the choice and use of substances and materials (Arbejdsmiljøfondet 1980: 25).

The actual functioning of the safety committees varies widely between enterprises. A recent study of the metal industry and the retail trade sector showed that 25 per cent of the establishments had not set up the prescribed safety group/committee at all (Langergaard 1991). In the majority of enterprises where an organization for health and safety does exist, the main problems seem to be the lack of systematic and preventive approaches and the lack of integration between health and safety work and technical management. The possibility for proactive intervention, by influencing the technological planning process at an early stage, seems to be exploited only in a small minority of firms (Kiil & Heide 1986; Aldrich 1988; Møller et al. 1988; Kofoed 1990).

New technology and participation

As already touched upon, questions arising from the introduction of new technology have played an important role in the Danish discussions on employee participation since the 1970s. With steeply rising unemployment figures from 1974, technological rationalizations became an issue of conflict as employees and trade unions tried to protect job security. Several prolonged strikes and bitter confrontations, notably in breweries and newspaper print shops, led to the first technology agreements regulating manning levels and employment protection in relation to the introduction of new technology. Other local agreements followed, and in 1981 the LO and DA concluded a general technology agreement which was later integrated into the Cooperation Agreement.

The provisions of the agreement made it mandatory for enterprises to assess the consequences of new technology and discuss them with employee representatives in the cooperation committee, and also to discuss the training needs arising from new technology. In the case of loss of jobs, the agreement obliged the employer to transfer employees to other jobs, if possible, or to support their retraining, thus improving their chances of getting a job elsewhere.

From the mid-1980s the qualitative aspects of new technology became more predominant in the relations between the two parties. Employers increasingly realized that the active participation of employees was useful if the potentials of the technology should be exploited; technical changes without the necessary adaptation of skills, work organization and motivation often gave disappointing results (Gjerding et al. 1990).

The trade unions, for their part, began to put greater stress on training, job content and participation. In 1991 the LO adopted a programme for 'personal growth in work' which aimed to improve the qualitative aspects of work by influencing the design of techniques and jobs (LO 1991a). In the years 1989–91 both peak organizations were actively involved in a state-financed initiative on 'management and cooperation in relation to technological innovation'. The aim of the initiative was to increase the competitiveness of Danish enterprises by strengthening both the direct and representative participation of employees in the decision-making process (Andersen 1991).

This initiative and similar projects in individual enterprises are examples of a tendency towards closer integration of employees and their representatives into the decision-making process. But a comprehensive involvement in the design of techniques, work organization and jobs remains relatively rare. Where and when it takes place, it usually occurs at the initiative of management, the primary function being to make the process of rationalization smoother. Proactive interventions, based on consciously formulated employee interests in relation to job content, training and working environment, are rare exceptions (Lorentzen 1990: 15, 28).

The position of trade unions and employers' organizations

Since the signing of the 1981 technology agreement, participation has not been a conflict issue to any significant degree between the two parties of the labour market. The employers' organizations now fully accept the existing institutions and, on this basis, take part in initiatives aiming to improve cooperation.

The trade union movement is also on the whole content with the existing provisions on participation. Yet, a comprehensive proposal for a reform of labour regulation, adopted by the LO congress by the end of 1991, included a number of demands intending to strengthen the representation and participation of workers' interests. Shop stewards are to be consulted in relation to recruitment, and a more clearly defined protection is demanded. The right to elect representatives to company boards shall be extended to all types of firms (today cooperative societies are not covered by the legislation). Stricter information procedures and more resources for training representatives are demanded in order to ensure that the agreed frames for cooperation are realized in practice. It is also proposed that the peace obligation should be removed from issues which today are defined as management prerogatives (LO 1991b: 8–29). At the same time as a strengthening of the representative participation structures is advocated, the proposal also underlines demands for more direct employee involvement in lower-level management decisions.

Finally, it must be mentioned that the Danish trade union movement has been pressing for binding regulations, in the Nordic countries as well as in the EU, on cooperation committees or works councils in multinational groups. The DA is opposed to such regulations (LO handlingsplan 1991; Simonsen 1991).

Conclusion

The Danish system of employee participation at workplace and company level is thoroughly rooted in a long tradition of cooperation between the industrial relations parties. Historically, cooperation was primarily an *obligation* of the employees and their representatives. The comprehensive peace obligation, and the duty of shop stewards to cooperate, mainly served as instruments for preventing radical demands and forms of action from taking place; they were not positive instruments for the involvement of workers in management decisions. However, the obligation to cooperate was made more mutual by the Cooperation Agreement in force since 1947, and by the laws enacted in the 1970s on representation on company boards and the establishment of health and safety committees. Still, the basis for cooperation remains asymmetrical as the employee representatives enjoy only limited powers in these institutions.

Formally, Danish participation rights are relatively weak: there are no real co-decision or co-determination rights based on labour legislation or collective agreements, and in general there is no right to strike in relation to management issues. Employee representatives may try to exploit the comprehensive consultation rights given to them, but in the end the employer has the right to decide. The actual content of participation, then, to a large extent becomes dependent on local factors: on the one hand, the commitment of managers to a participative management style, and on the other, the priority given to participation by employees, their representatives and their trade unions. The success of the institutions established for participation thus depends heavily on voluntarism. This voluntarism, however, should not be confused with volatility. The strong and stable organizations of the Danish labour market, and their commitment to relations based on cooperation rather than confrontation, provide an influential framework for actions at the local level. This framework – more than the formal rules – explains the relatively important role played by participation in Danish work-place industrial relations.

The Cooperation Agreement (as well as board-level representation) was initially met by scepticism from employers. But labour market pressures in the 1960s, and technological and other pressures in the 1980s, have gradually made the employers more interested in exploiting the productive potentials of cooperation and participation. Trade unions have also shown a greater interest in participation, seeing it as a way of influencing job design, training and other conditions related to the qualitative aspects of working life. The result has been an increase over the past decade not just in the number of committees but also in the importance of the issues discussed.

Since the beginning of the 1970s, employee representatives have been able to participate in management decisions through four different channels: (a) the co-operation committee; (b) the safety groups and health and safety committee; (c) the company board; and (d) the more or less informal meetings between shop stewards and managers. Given the high degree of overlap of personnel, with the same shop stewards often seated on all the relevant bodies, employee representatives have good opportunities for furthering the views of employees, although the more proactive aspects of these possibilities are rarely fully exploited. Thus, for example, the provisions for an early participation of the cooperation committee and the health and safety committee in the planning of technical and organizational change only seldom materialize into conscious and active employee intervention in the planning process. This can undoubtedly be related both to the lack of a tradition of employee initiative in relation to management issues of a strategic or tactical nature, and to the absence of real co-decision powers. But, as noted by Lorentzen (1990), the fragmentation of participation, caused by the existence of several different participation channels, may also play a role. The treatment of different aspects in separate bodies makes it difficult for employee representatives to relate to the totality of consequences of a given management strategy or plan.

6

European Participation: Diverse Solutions to Common Problems

After the presentation of the country profiles in the preceding four chapters, it is now time to ask the crucial question: is there anything *European* about employee participation as it appears in Britain, Denmark, Spain and Germany? Is at all meaningful to speak of a specific European tradition and a possible European model within this particular area? This chapter will begin to address these questions by comparing the country-specific participation traditions and structures. The focus will thus still mainly be on *national* developments and institutions: similarities and diversities between the four countries under consideration. Chapters 7 and 8 will then continue the search for a European type of participation by focusing on *supranational* forces and institutions.

The common legacy

The participation of workers and other employees in management decisions through their elected representatives is a well-established phenomenon in all four countries under discussion. Management prerogatives are limited not only by labour legislation and collective agreements but also, within the framework created by legislation and collective bargaining, by institutions whose purpose it is to secure a degree of employee participation in management decisions at workplace and company level. Basically, all the countries have established institutions which imply a certain degree of departure from a unilateral management style, and the historical analyses point out that organized labour has been the driving force in the processes leading to this result. Either the labour movement has obtained participation powers directly through negotiation with employers, as is the case for the most important participatory institutions in Denmark and for considerable parts of the British labour market, or it has appeared so politically powerful and challenging that governments have found it opportune to legislate comprehensively on employee participation, as is the case for Germany and Spain.

The British finding (Daniel 1987) that both direct and indirect participation is more widespread in unionized than non-unionized firms very well illustrates a common basis for European employee participation, namely the aspirations of workers and their trade unions to gain influence over the conditions under which they work. Further, it is notable that even in participation systems based on the principle of unitary representation, systems which in their origin were conceived as a means to curb trade union power, most seats on the participatory bodies are filled by trade union members and activists. The German *Betriebsrat,* as designed under the Weimar Republic, and the *jurado de empresa* of the Franco dictatorship were instruments aiming to weaken or render superfluous the trade union movement. Today, the works councils of these countries function as *de facto* extensions of trade union organizations (Müller-Jentsch 1986; Martín Valverde et al. 1991). In the search for a common European model, the strong stamp of trade unionism cannot be ignored. The development of participation into a mechanism for social integration and workplace regulation has taken place in a dialectical interplay between governments and the trade union movement. This is the general conclusion for the period since the Second World War, with Franco's Spain and Britain since 1979 as exceptions to the rule.

Studies of the historical development of employee participation in different countries lend support to the theory that sees both interest in participation and its growth as elapsing in cycles rather than as an evolutionary process (Ramsay 1983). For Germany, Britain and Denmark it is even possible to identify a common cyclical pattern, with boom periods in the years after the two world wars and in the 1970s, and slump or stagnation in the other parts of the century. The three boom periods were all, and in all of the three countries, characterized by crises in the pre-existing modes of capitalist domination, and by rising expectations and demands on the part of the labour movement.

Looking at the development in the four countries and in the EU countries in general, it is, however, also evident that labour's historical march for more collective influence at the workplace has been halted, at least for the time being. The 1970s saw a significant increase in employee participation rights: in Denmark, legislation on health and safety committees and board-level representation; in Germany, extension of the rights of works councils, and a stronger representation on supervisory boards in large companies; in Spain, the preparation for comprehensive workers' rights under the post-Franco constitution; and in Britain, legislation on representation on health and safety committees. But since 1980 there has been virtually no increase in employee participation rights, except for Spain where some limited changes took place in 1984 (participation rights of shop stewards).

To some extent the shift that took place around 1980 might be explained by the simultaneous shift in the colour of governments. In

Britain, Denmark and Germany, governments dominated by Social Democratic or Labour parties were replaced by governments lead by Conservatives or Christian Democrats. While the Thatcher government of Britain was directly hostile towards trade unions and collective employee rights, the Danish and German governments seemed on the whole to be satisfied with the status quo. Yet, the German Kohl government did attempt to weaken the influence of mainstream trade unionism in 1989 by changing the procedures for works council elections. Conversely, participation rights were extended in Spain under the socialist government (as it was in socialist-governed France too, with the introduction of the Auroux laws in 1982; Gold & Hall 1990).

It may be that the possible advent of socialist governments in the future will unleash new rounds of extended participation. But, right or left, governments are also influenced by wider ideological currents and international shifts in business and market conditions. The general growth of representative forms of participation during the 1970s must be seen *partly* as a response to radical workers' demands, built up during the end of the long post-war boom and its conditions of full employment, exploding in 1968–75 in mass strikes and factory occupations notably in Italy, France, Britain and Spain. Participation was a trade union and government response aimed at integrating the radical working-class currents into the system through institutional channels. *Partly* the increase in participation was an element in a wider strategy to combat the economic crisis which hit Europe as well as other parts of the world from 1973 onwards. The response of most European governments to this situation was initially to strengthen and extend existing corporatist decision-making structures; the different interest groups moved closer together at the national level in order to find common solutions to depressed business and employment conditions (Streeck 1984). Corporatism, i.e. a close cooperation and coordination between the state and the two labour market parties, was an ideological concept supported by socialists, conservatives and leading industrialists. While corporatism meant more trade union participation in political and administrative decisions at societal level, it was also conducive to an extension of the legal rights of participation at the company and workplace level.

However, as the corporatist strategies, at least for some countries, failed to produce the hoped-for return to prosperity and full employment, they were gradually weakened and then replaced by strategies building on completely different ideas, namely liberalist doctrines. These strategies saw excessive regulation and state intervention as the causes of economic stagnation which at that time was termed 'Eurosclerosis'. Consequently, deregulation, flexibility and the return to a higher degree of management autarchy were advocated as the central means of overcoming the problems. The catchwords became: more market, less state; more flexibility, less regulation (Hyman 1990).

Employee participation based on collective rights and representation was seen as one of several unwanted obstacles to managerial freedom; and in so far as participation stayed on the employers' agenda, it was in the form of direct participation based on unilateral management initiatives, e.g. group work and quality circles, often connected with wider human resource strategies or in imitation of Japanese management concepts. Although the data are very incomplete, it seems safe to conclude that since the beginning of the 1980s there has been an increase in such forms of direct employee involvement in all the four countries studied.

The international movement for economic liberalism was spearheaded by Thatcher's Britain and Reagan's USA, but it is hardly an exaggeration to say that by the mid-1980s this ideological current was making its influence felt on all the governments within the European Community. The political adoption of the liberalizations leading to the EC single market was the most outstanding illustration of this.

So, not just the colour of governments, but the whole economic–political–ideological conjuncture is decisive for the development or not of employee participation. Since the mid-1970s the position of employees and trade unions has been relatively weak because of the impact of mass unemployment, and since 1980 the ideology of liberalism, deregulation and managerial unilateralism has been predominant. These are the main factors for explaining why the historical trend for progressive extensions of formally recognized participation rights has come to a halt.

For the moment it remains to be seen whether the weakening of the British Conservative government, pressures for a higher degree of consensus within companies and new trends in management philosophy are signalling the end of the ideology of deregulation and unilateral management power. A new cycle may be under way. It very much depends on whether the European Union in the coming years can agree, ideologically and politically, on an industrial strategy which sees organized labour as an asset rather than a constraint.

National peculiarities

The identification above of a common legacy – stemming from trade unionism as a common dynamic, and from specific supranational forces which have influenced the overall cyclical development of European employee participation – was only possible by looking at employee participation from a relatively high level of abstraction. On the more concrete levels of analysis, the differences between the four national systems of employee participation are much more conspicuous than the similarities. Each of the four systems has its own distinctive features representing specific national compromises, historically worked out as attempts to strike a balance between the industrial relations parties.

The German system was established in the periods after the two world wars when the economic as well as political system of the country was in deep crisis, and when the labour movement found itself in a strong position; the Spanish system was born out of similar circumstances in the post-Franco transition period. In class terms, the formalized participation structures of both countries arose from situations where the bourgeois forces were severely compromised and divided, and where the labour movement correspondingly found a larger space for manoeuvre.

In Britain and Denmark, such critical historical 'moments of truth' have been less marked, and so have their results as far as employee participation is concerned. In both countries, the labour movement sought to change the balance of power in the aftermath of the two world wars (parallel to and partly inspired by events in Germany), but the Danish cooperation committees remain the only lasting result from these periods. Likewise, the labour offensive of the late 1960s and 1970s produced different results in the four countries. While employee and trade union participation rights were extended in Germany, Denmark and Spain, much less happened in Britain where the Bullock approach for institutionalizing participation failed to be adopted.

In the following we shall look more closely at some of the characteristics distinguishing the four systems and at factors which may explain why the countries have chosen diverse solutions.

Legislation versus voluntarism

Employee participation in Germany and Spain is based on detailed legislation, while statutory regulation is almost totally absent in Britain, and Denmark has a mixture of legal and voluntary regulation. Sometimes these differences are ascribed to the different national character traits or cultures of European peoples: the formal Germans, the informal British etc., but such an explanation is hardly satisfying: are Germans and Spaniards really more like each other than Germans and Danes?

In a sociological perspective it appears that dependence on legislation is connected with corporatist social and political traditions, whereas voluntarism is related to pluralist and liberalist traditions. But underneath these differences the extent and content of labour legislation within a given society must be understood as the result of major problems and contradictions which historically have arisen within it. In this perspective, German and Spanish legislation may be explained as attempts by the state to reconcile interests whose open warfare seriously disrupted the functioning of the economy as well as the social order. In other words, the 'legalism' of the Spanish and German systems derives from the fact that, historically, the labour movements in these countries have been sufficiently radical and powerful to be conceived as a major threat to the capitalist order (cf. the periods after the two world wars in Germany, the Civil War and the post-Franco transition period in Spain).

The smaller role played by legislation in Britain and Denmark may be explained along similar lines. The British labour movement has never severely threatened the social order as a political force. Only as a response to periods of widespread radicalism among sections of the working class, such as during and after the First World War and in the 1970s, have British governments seriously considered introducing legal participation rights. In Denmark, the story is more mixed. In 1947 a threat of legislation was behind the central collective agreement on cooperation committees, whereas the growing radicalism of the early 1970s was actually followed by legislation on health and safety committees and representation at board level. Yet, the most important institutions for employee participation rest on collective agreements.

The voluntarism of Britain and Denmark reflects the fact that employers and trade unions in these countries reached a direct compromise relatively early, recognizing each other as bargaining agents and settling matters in a way which by and large was acceptable to the wider society. In Germany and Spain, on the contrary, class antagonism was stronger and the wills of the parties more contradictory: legal regulations were introduced because voluntarism, seen from the viewpoint of the state, did not function. Under Hitler and Franco the state response was repression of the labour movement; under the subsequent democratic constitutions it has been to strike a compromise between those employer and employee interests which earlier appeared antagonistic.

Unitary versus trade union representation at workplace level

From a formal point of view there is a great difference between Spain and Germany on the one hand, and Denmark and Britain on the other, regarding the main institutions for participation at workplace level. The Spanish and German works councils are unitary bodies elected by all employees irrespective of trade union membership. Contrary to this, the Danish and British shop steward institutions, which are essential to participation in these countries, are based on elections only among trade union members. The employee side of joint consultation bodies (in Denmark cooperation committees, in Britain joint consultative committees) are also normally filled by shop stewards, although the increasing number of non-unionized workplaces in Britain constitute an important exception.

Yet, in reality, the difference between unitary and trade union representation is much less marked. Even though the introduction of works councils by the state historically aimed at weakening trade unionism, for which reason the German trade union movement and the dominant Spanish trade unions were originally hostile to such bodies, works councils constitute today a *de facto* part of trade unionism in the two countries. The great majority of works council members are also trade union members and they are elected on trade union candidate lists. In fact, the works councils give the trade unions greater influence at workplace level than could be expected from membership density. The most obvious example of this is Spain where works councils exist in about 75 per cent of eligible places and about 90 per cent of the works council seats are held by trade union members, in spite of an average trade union membership of just 15 per cent. Thus, trade union presence in terms of workplaces covered by trade unionists with the authority to represent the workforce, is broader than in Britain where trade union membership is around 40 per cent, but where at the same time about half of the establishments do not recognize trade unions (Martín Valverde 1991; Millward et al. 1992).

The argument, however, might be turned around. It is plausible to suggest that the securing of employee rights through works council legislation reduces the motivation of employees to join a trade union. Again Spain is the most marked example. The works councils are granted a wide range of powers, including monitoring existing regulative rules, taking legal action, calling strikes and conducting collective bargaining. This certainly makes trade union membership less obvious seen from the perspective of the individual employee. At the same time, Spanish labour legislation strongly favours the most representative unions, i.e. the unions which obtain most seats at the works council elections. In this sense, the power of Spanish trade unions is directly dependent upon the success they enjoy in the works council system. Martín Valverde (1991) refers to this as a 'voters' trade unionism' in contrast to the members' trade unionism seen in other countries.

Regarding trade union membership, Denmark is at the other extreme with approximately 90 per cent of employees organized. The high rate is connected to the fact that Danish trade unions participate in a whole range of decisions at societal level (health and safety regulation, vocational training, employment schemes, the administration of unemployment funds etc.) which in other national systems are often administered unilaterally by the public authorities or the employers (Lind 1991). One might call Danish trade unionism a 'citizens' unionism': it is as common to be a member of a trade union as to vote at parliamentary or local elections, but only a minor fraction of the members are active in trade union activities, including elections (Andersen et al. 1993).

To sum up: the difference between the unitary representation principle and the trade union principle is not decisive for the extent and intensity of participation developed in practice. The choice of one or other, however, has left significant marks on the total national industrial relations system, including the type of trade unionism which has become predominant in the individual countries.

Board-level representation

Historically, participation at company level through representation on company or supervisory boards was first initiated by government (in Germany in 1922). Shortly afterwards, the idea was taken up by the German trade union movement in connection with the formulation of the demand for equality between capital and labour at all levels of society, and in a form where participation should take place through trade union representatives rather than representatives elected by all employees. Later, demands for this type of participation spread to other national trade union movements.

With the exception of the period under Hitler, German employees have had admission to the board rooms since 1922. In Denmark, participation at board level has been in force since 1973. In Britain and Spain, on the contrary, there are no statutory provisions for board-level representation. This may partly be explained by the fact that the trade union movements of these countries have, until recently, been opposed to this form of participation on the grounds that it endangers the independence of trade union and employee interests.

Here again we find a clear formal difference, now with Germany and Denmark in one camp, Spain and Britain in the other. And again the difference seems to be of no great significance in practice. There are no indications that the participation at board level of Danish and German employee representatives has led to changes in the overall decisions or priorities of the companies, not even in the German *Montanindustrie* which is the only place where the employee side holds a position of full parity or co-determination.

On the other hand, one should not underestimate the more invisible consequences of board-level representation. There is hardly any doubt that this institution increases the mutual information and understanding between the two parties, thus promoting a more trustful industrial relations climate less prone to conflict. At the same time, the relatively undramatic experience of participation at board level has defused the original attitudes of the parties to this issue. Danish and German trade unions no longer give a high priority to campaigns for extended board-level representation in the expectation of thereby obtaining great changes in favour of labour, and the employers who originally were strongly opposed to this attack on the prerogatives of owners and managers have accommodated to the changed situation. To them, board-level participation is acceptable, maybe even desirable, as long as it does not amount to full parity representation.

Still, the German *Montanindustrie*, in spite of the fact that it is diminishing for structural reasons, may again become the model for demands for extended participation and industrial democracy. The combination at board level of 'equality between capital and labour' and representatives of the wider society is one type of structural solution which points beyond the democratic and ecological deficits produced by a capitalism based entirely on owner interests.

Bodies for interest representation or the creation of consensus?

Participation is a multidimensional phenomenon. It may be wanted by employees, employers and governments alike, but for different purposes. Concerning the participation institutions of the four European countries under study, one may ask: do the institutions mainly serve as instruments for the furthering of collective employee interests? Or, do they primarily serve as a forum for the working out of consensus decisions between representatives of the workforce and management? More specifically: are the bodies suitable for obtaining compromises where both parties get an advantage (plus-sum game), or do they tend to foster solutions where one party gains at the expense of the other? And finally: how does the general national industrial relations climate of the countries colour the functioning of the participation institutions?

In *Britain*, the shop steward institution is inscribed in a setting where relations between employers and employees is traditionally perceived as adversarial, or as the co-existence of opposing interests. Collective bargaining is the traditional, and at some workplaces the only, way used to reach agreement between the two sides. The main function of the shop steward is to serve the interests of the workers, not to take part in management decisions. When employers propose changes, shop stewards will typically react by asking for negotiations with management in order to try to influence the changes and their consequences on the shopfloor. Studies (Clegg 1976; Daniel & Millward 1984) show that, at least in some companies, shop stewards bargain over issues which in other systems are normally dealt with through formalized consultation or co-decision procedures. Only in a minority of British workplaces are there bodies specifically established for participation purposes. The mainstream of British participation is therefore taking place in a reactive and rather narrow perspective of serving the members here and now. The structure promotes compromises seen in a zero-sum perspective rather than a broader consensus based on a plus-sum perspective. The sights of shop stewards are influenced by the lack of guaranteed participation rights on the one hand, and access to a relatively unlimited right to strike on the other.

While the emphasis put on the defence of employee interests in Britain may be seen as a consequence of the insecurity fostered by voluntarism, the defensiveness of *Spanish* employee participation is codified by labour law. The Spanish works councils are conceived as first and foremost bodies whose purpose it is to represent and defend the interests of workers. This is underlined by the rights granted to them, especially the right to call strikes, the right to enter into collective bargaining, and the right to monitor existing labour regulations. The rights to information, consultation and co-decision are also formulated as defensive instruments rather than instruments for an active cooperation between the two parties. For instance, Spanish labour legislation presents the works council's participation rights and its obligation to cooperate as completely separate areas, and consultation rights are framed as a right to be heard on specific issues rather than to discuss them with management in an active way (Martín Valverde et al. 1991). The Spanish participation system thus reflects the tradition for adversarial or even antagonistic relationships between employers and workers – at the same time as it strikes a compromise by defining in detail the powers of the respective parties.

The *German* Works Constitution includes some strong elements furthering consensus decisions. There is no strike right for the works councils but, conversely, there are relatively significant co-decision rights which impel the two parties to reach agreement, directly or with the help of an outside conciliator. Yet, this does not prevent the works council provisions from also containing powerful instruments for the promotion of traditional collective employee interests. The German system promotes consensus decisions and cooperation between the parties, but on premises which put employee interests in a clearly stronger position than in almost all other industrial relations systems. The cooperative character of the relations is further strengthened by the fact that collective bargaining is defined as lying outside the scope of the works councils.

Finally, the *Danish* system is again more mixed. The main function of the shop stewards is to represent and further collective employee interests. However, at the same time they are obliged by collective agreement to cooperate with the employer and they have only very limited rights concerning industrial action. The joint cooperation committees have mere consultative functions, but aim actively at creating consensus decisions on principles related to employment and working conditions. Cooperation is also supported by strong corporatist structures at industry and national level. All in all, there are strong features in the Danish system working in favour of consensus decisions, but because of a lack of real co-decision rights the cooperation is more employer dominated than in the German case.

To sum up: the employee participation structures of Spain and Britain are primarily seen and used as instruments for furthering the collective interests of employees within a zero-sum logic, whereas in Denmark and Germany they are more prone to lead to processes of cooperation and consensus decision-making where the exchange between the two parties is perceived in a plus-sum perspective. These differences are related to variations in the design of the national participation systems but also to influences from the wider industrial relations traditions and structures of the different countries. In Spain and Britain there are strong traditions for contestation and collective bargaining as the predominant forms of exchange, while corporatist types of exchange are much more rooted in Denmark and Germany (cf. Crouch 1993).

As can be seen from figure 6.1 overt labour conflict clearly plays a larger role in Spain and Britain than in Denmark and especially Germany. It would be too hasty a conclusion to interpret the diverse national conflict levels as reflections of the respective participation systems; rather, they mirror the industrial relations systems at large. On the other hand, it is not difficult to discern features of the German and Danish participation systems which favour a low conflict level. The representation at board level, and the whole range of conflict-mitigating procedures surrounding the German works councils and the Danish cooperation committees are institutional frameworks which over time have promoted dialogue and mutual understanding between the two parties. This again increases the visibility of plus-sum options and reduces the attractiveness of conflict.

Formal participation rights versus actual participation and influence

Is there a direct correlation between formal participation rights, on the one hand, and the degree of actual participation and influence on the other? As illustrated several times in chapters 2–5, it is possible that formal participation rights are not adhered to in practice, and,

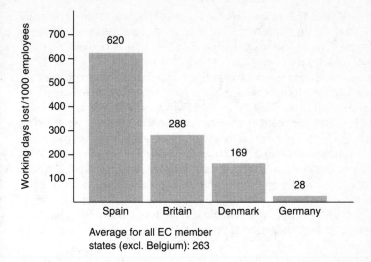

Figure 6.1 *Labour conflict in Spain, Britain, Denmark and Germany, average working days lost per 1000 employees 1981–90 (Employment Observatory 1992)*

conversely, that participation is developed and practised irrespective of formal regulations. In addition, influence may be obtained by other methods than participation.

As for *formal* participation rights, it is not an impossible task to compare and rank the four countries in relation to each other. This is done in table 6.1 on the basis of the existing national regulations (legislation and central collective agreements) on the issue. At both the company and workplace level, formal rights are strongest in Germany. At the company level, Spain and Britain share the bottom position because neither of the countries has provisions for participation of this type. As for the workplace level, Britain is again at the bottom while Denmark and Spain share a middle position. Consultation rights are of a stronger character in Denmark than in Spain inasmuch as the explicit aim of Danish cooperation committees is to reach agreement (although the employer is only obliged to discuss, not actually to conclude joint

Table 6.1 *Rank order of countries on formal participation rights of employee representatives*

	Workplace level	Company level
Germany	1	1
Denmark	2–3	2
Spain	2–3	3–4
Britain	4	3–4

decisions), whereas the consultation rights of Spanish works councils mainly take the much more passive form of the submission of opinions. On the other hand, the, admittedly weak, co-decision rights of Spanish workers have no parallel in the Danish provisions.

An assessment of the *actual* participation practised and enjoyed by employee representatives is much more complicated as there is a lack of sufficiently strong sociological evidence for a comparative analysis. For Germany, there is evidence that works councils are actually confined to a minority of workplaces and that the formal powers are not being utilized in a substantial number of enterprises (Müller-Jentsch 1986; Weiss 1987). For Britain, conversely, it has been shown that shop stewards often have more influence than could be expected from studying legislation and collective agreements (Clegg 1976; Daniel & Millward 1984). But especially for Spain and Denmark, there is an almost complete lack of systematic knowledge about the actual functioning of the participation systems.

The only comparative study which throws light on the differences in actual participation between the four countries is the EC survey conducted in 1987–88 by the European Foundation. The main focus of the study was the participation of employee representatives in decisions concerning the introduction of new technology (see chapter 8), but participation in other areas, including work organization, was also analysed. The study distinguished between four levels of intensity of participation, namely (a) no involvement; (b) information; (c) consultation; and (d) negotiation or joint decision-making. For decisions related to technology and work organization, Germany and Denmark could be singled out as the two EC member states which had the highest intensity of participation (a relatively high frequency of negotiation or joint decision-making). Britain fell in a middle group with consultation as the prominent participation method, while Spain was placed in a group of mainly southern European countries where 'no involvement' or 'information only' were the most frequently used practices (Fröhlich et al. 1991; Gill & Krieger 1992). Table 6.2 gives a rough overview of the results for the four countries concerning participation in decisions related to work organization.

From actual participation to actual influence there is again a step. Participation takes place within environments which are more or less dominated by employers, and its weaker forms, information and consultation, do not necessarily yield any influence; furthermore, influence can be obtained through other channels than participation, such as collective agreements or informal shopfloor activities. A study undertaken by the IDE International Research Group in the late 1970s attempted to take this into account and to compare the actual influence enjoyed by workers and their representative bodies in different European

Table 6.2 *Most frequent intensity of participation in decisions on work organization*

	Negotiation or joint decisions	Consultation	Information	No participation
Germany	X			
Denmark	X			
Britain		X		
Spain				X

The table is based on responses from an equal number of managers and employee representatives.
Source: Gill & Krieger 1992

countries (IDE 1981). Table 6.3 shows the results for Germany, Britain and Denmark; unfortunately, Spain was not included in the study.

While workers in all three countries were close to the level of 'little influence', the variations were greater among the representative bodies. German bodies approached the level of 'moderate influence', and the British bodies, maybe surprisingly, had more influence than the Danish ones. But, as noted by Lane (1989), the British figures would probably have been somewhat lower if the study had been repeated ten years later.

In general, it is not possible to explain these findings on influence as being caused by differences in formal participation rights between the three countries. Yet it is difficult to find other explanations for the high German score for representative bodies than the strong legal rights enjoyed by German employee representatives.

A safe conclusion regarding the relations between formal participation rights, actual participation and actual influence cannot be reached on the basis of the evidence available. The findings for Germany, and to some extent Denmark, do seem to indicate a correlation between

Table 6.3 *Degree of influence of workers and representative bodies*

	Workers	Representative bodies
Germany	1.9	2.6
Britain	2.0	2.2
Denmark	2.0	1.9

1, no influence; 2, little influence; 3, moderate influence; 4, much influence; 5, very much influence. Respondents were asked to rate their amount of influence in relation to 16 issues for decision-making concerning working and employment conditions.

Source: IDE 1981

formal participation rights and actual participation and influence. The results for Spain pull in the other direction, but here it must be remembered that the Spanish participation system is of relatively recent origin and was introduced into an industrial relations system marked by conflict and autocratic management traditions. A cautious conclusion would be that formal rights do matter – but it takes time!

Reactive or proactive participation?

None of the four systems of employee participation was designed with the purpose of obtaining a situation where management functions are shared equally between owners and employees. Although the German trade union movement, in particular, has fought for the realization of full co-determination, this concept has not been implemented anywhere, except at the level of supervisory boards in the German *Montanindustrie*. Rather, what has happened is that labour has been assigned a role as junior partner (Germany) or controller (Spain) in relation to management decisions related to employment and working conditions. To manage is still the prerogative of the owners, and both parties still expect initiatives for change to come from management, not just regarding changes at the strategic and tactical but also at the operational level. And so they do, leaving it to the employee representatives to react to these changes.

Yet, especially in Denmark and Germany, there is evidence of a more proactive type of participation on the part of employee representatives – in relation to issues such as the introduction of new technology, training, job design and work organization. Not that the initiatives for change come from the employee representatives – this is indeed still rare – but it has become more usual that representatives are consulted at an early phase, and are allowed to take part, in a thorough and comprehensive way, in the discussion of alternative solutions and the planning of changes. This may take place through the general bodies for participation or through specific project groups or working committees.

Such proactive approaches are only realistic within companies with strong relations of trust and where both parties have built up experience with plus-sum results based on mutual respect and cooperation. In turn, the proactive involvement of employees may strongly extend the scope of participation and give it a much more constructive meaning: instead of participation being essentially a defensive instrument for monitoring management initiatives, it now becomes a means for employees actively to influence the design of changes at the workplace.

Virtuous circles for participation of a proactive style are most likely to develop within industrial relations systems where traditions of corporatism and cooperation are strong. This was confirmed by the IDE study which found that employee involvement, especially at the strategic level, was strongly connected to the institutionalization of participation (IDE 1981: 126). So, it is not surprising that the earlier quoted EC study showed that participation at an early stage of the decision-making process, in the planning phase, was considerably more common in Denmark and Germany than in Britain and Spain (Fröhlich et al. 1991: 152).

Conclusion: the persistence of national institutions

If we now leave the actual functioning of the participation systems aside and turn to the institutions as such, it is striking, first, that once institutions have been established they tend to be reinforced by developments at the national arena, and, secondly, that institutions are not easily borrowed from foreign industrial relations systems.

The *British* shop steward institution was established by the trade unions and workers themselves. In the absence of statutory regulation on employee representation and participation, the shop stewards have remained by far the most important mouthpiece for employees at workplace level. It was in line with this tradition that the 1974 legislation on participation in relation to health and safety provided for trade union rather than unitary representation. Conversely, the ambitious attempt at importing parity representation at board level from the German tradition (the 1977 Bullock proposal) failed to be implemented.

In *Germany*, the introduction of statutory works councils from 1920 and their reintroduction after the Second World War laid the foundation for a wholly different representation and participation model. Here, it was the attempts by trade unions to establish a strong shop steward representation which failed. Instead, the trade unions adapted to the works council institution by more or less conquering it. The representation on supervisory boards is also a persistent feature of German industrial relations.

In *Denmark*, we see a combination of 'British' and 'German' elements. Shop stewards play a significant role, partly simply as shop stewards, and partly in their capacity of having priority to the employee seats on the joint cooperation committees. Here, the principle of trade union representation is predominant. The employee representatives at board level, on the other hand, are elected according to the unitary principle; and, as for safety representatives, the law mixes the two principles in a peculiar way: the law applies to all workplaces above a certain size irrespective of trade union organization, but for election procedures and protection against dismissal it refers to the rules concerning shop stewards – rules which are determined by collective bargaining. The introduction of cooperation committees in 1947, as well as board-level representation in 1973, was inspired by German institutions, but it must be noted that in contrast to the German works councils the Danish cooperation committees are based on collective agreement and are joint management–employee bodies.

In *Spain*, finally, the system created since the late 1970s centres around the unitary representation principle. Although there are obvious similarities to the German works councils, more fundamentally the Spanish system represents a continuity of the works councils existing under the Franco regime, and, even more important, of the forms of struggle against this regime undertaken notably by the *comisiones obreras*. The fact that the Spanish works councils are empowered with the right to strike and to negotiate collective agreements distinguishes them significantly from the German system, and also from the institutions of the Franco era.

As can be seen, each of the different participation systems represents specific national trajectories. In the course of history, some elements have been inspired by or borrowed from foreign industrial relations systems. However, to a very important extent, changes within each country have built on and adapted to already existing national institutions and traditions, thus reinforcing these. So, on the basis of the evidence presented so far, there seem to be no strong tendencies for a convergence between national participation arrangements within the European Union. It can be seen that the national institutions have, historically, been influenced to a significant degree by common determinants, and have moved through common cycles. But the concrete outcomes of these determinants and cycles diverge from country to country; in each country there have been powerful tendencies supporting already existing institutions, whereby national diversity has been cemented.

At the same time, the national histories also remind us that institutional changes, even radical ones, do take place from time to time, and most certainly will also take place in the future. The existing institutions are best understood as the outcomes or compromises emerging from specific situations of crisis in the relationship between capital and labour in the respective countries. As noted already, it is possible to distinguish the years immediately after the two world wars and the late 1960s and early 1970s as periods of crisis for at least three of the four countries, and periods when steps were taken to extend participation in all these countries. The question is whether future crises will also be met by mainly national responses, or whether the European Union is by now so politically and economically integrated that the response will primarily be European in character.

A final point, which it is important to make here, is that the approach chosen so far has undoubtedly under-rated the role of possible factors pushing in the direction of convergence. By focusing on national rather than supranational scenes some significant tendencies at play may have been omitted or underestimated. So, before making any final conclusions as to the (un)likelihood of a future convergence of the forms and intensity of employee participation across the EU member states, it is necessary to look closer into how forces operating at a supranational level affect participation. The next two chapters will analyse the roles played by the European Union and technology respectively.

The European Union: the Long March towards Common Regulations

This chapter deals with the initiatives and debates within the European Union/Community concerning EU-wide regulations of the form and content of employee participation in companies and groups of companies. The first section attempts briefly to provide an overview of the objectives of EU policy in this area and the phases it has run through. The following sections treat the different initiatives taken: the grand plans as well as the heated debates and the modest results.

EU policies: objectives and phases

European Community initiatives on employee participation date back to the 1960s. It was not primarily concerns over industrial relations that prompted the Commission to take up the question. Rather it was brought up as a side-issue to the attempt to create uniform conditions for companies operating within the Community. A harmonization of the existing company laws of the member states, and the establishment of a set of rules for 'European' companies, were seen by the Commission as necessary steps towards a genuine common market and a strengthening of European competitiveness *vis-à-vis* American multinational companies (Dowdy 1990).

There were two basic assumptions behind the Commission's taking up employee participation in connection with a harmonization of company legislation. The first had to do with the market: in order to operate under equal conditions, companies must be subject to, among other things, equal rules regarding employee participation. The second was more political and related to the desired role of companies in society. Here, the Commission was influenced by the change in company law philosophy occurring around 1970. Instead of being just a means of profit maximization in the interest of shareholders, with labour only appearing in an external contractual relationship, the company now tended to be seen as an institution which should at the same time serve the interests of the capital owners, the employees and society as a whole. This 'harmony model' was well developed in Germany and also inspired a revision of Dutch company law in 1971 (Schmitthoff 1977).

The objective of harmonizing company law was, from the turbulent late 1960s, accompanied by pressure from Germany in particular for a more active social policy within the Community (George 1991; Springer 1992). This resulted in the Commission working out in 1973 a Social Action Programme in which one of the sections dealt specifically with participation and industrial democracy (CEC 1974). Among its aims, adopted by the Council the following year, were 'progressively to involve workers or their representatives in the life of undertakings in the Community' and 'to develop the involvement of management and labour in the economic and social decisions of the Community' (Council Resolution 1974).

Thus, the course was set for European industrial relations of a corporatist type: the rights and social position of labour were to be secured by the Community, and legislation and other initiatives should facilitate a close cooperation between capital and labour ranging from company to Community level. Participation should be based on legal rights and be safeguarded in national as well as multinational companies.

Yet, corporatism flourished more in the individual member states than at the EC level. Protectionist attitudes and national differences prevented the adoption of most of the measures projected in the 1974 action programme, and from around 1980 the political situation changed markedly. The election of Margaret Thatcher in Britain and Ronald Reagan in the US signalled a shift from corporatist to neo-liberalist ideas. The neo-liberalists insisted that a revival of the economy was dependent upon a removal of barriers to 'free enterprise', including barriers to the employers' unilateral right to manage. To them the slow growth of the European economy was due to a special disease, 'Euro-sclerosis', which they claimed was caused notably by excessive state regulation and trade union influence. From then on the EC became a battleground where 'corporatists' and 'neo-liberalists' were fighting for radically different kinds of solutions, and where social policy had cumbersome conditions given the fact that decisions required unanimity in the Council of Ministers. Only the adoption of the Maastricht Treaty which entered into force in November 1993 changed this situation.

Neo-liberalism, however, never got strong enough to change the political priorities of the EC completely. It is true that the plans for creating a liberalized internal market altered the course drastically. These plans originated from the big European capitalists meeting in the Roundtable of European Industrialists, and they were endorsed by the Commission in its White Paper of 1985 (CEC 1985). Basically, the internal market project was the liberalist medicine corresponding to the liberalist diagnosis of 'Euro-sclerosis'. But, ironically enough, it was exactly this project which put the question of employee participation and other social issues back on the EC agenda (Venturini 1988; Betten 1991; Springer 1992).

In 1985 the European Trade Union Confederation (ETUC) decided to give its support to the internal market on the condition that it would be supplemented by social measures paying attention to labour interests (Lapeyre 1990). The Commission, and in particular its president, the French socialist Jacques Delors, as well as the European Parliament, also strongly advocated a 'social dimension' to the internal market. The arguments for a social dimension were that it would guarantee that the expected gains from liberalization would not only benefit capital but also the working population, and that this was necessary in order to secure broad support for the project. The eventual outcome of these discussions was the Community Charter on Fundamental Social Rights of Workers adopted by the Council (minus Britain) in December 1989, and the related Action Programme (CEC 1990a, b). Among the measures announced here were the preparation of a new initiative on workers' participation as well as the revival of an earlier proposal.

The charter and the action programme were welcomed by the ETUC whereas the employer organization at European level, UNICE, expressed severe reservations. UNICE found that the Commission proposed legislation in areas, such as information, consultation and participation of employees, which ought to be left entirely to collective bargaining or national legislation (Tyszkiewicz 1990).

However, the work of implementing the ideas of the social charter and its action programme progressed very slowly. When the magic date for the completion of the internal market, New Year 1992/93, arrived, hardly anything had been decided in the social and industrial relations area. This was mainly due to opposition from the British government and the delayed ratification of the Maastricht Treaty in Denmark, Britain and Germany. The latter meant a postponement of the introduction of qualified majority voting on social policy measures.

In the following we shall look more closely at the initiatives taken by the European Commission within the field of employee participation. The most important initiatives are the proposals for a European Company Statute, the Fifth Directive on company harmonization, the 'Vredeling' Directive, and the European Works Councils Directive.

The European Company Statute

Shortly after the formation of the EEC the Commission found it important for the common market to be accompanied by a common legal framework for companies located within the Community. In order to achieve this objective the Commission worked out proposals for the harmonization of the different national company laws (see next section), but it also embarked on the more radical approach of establishing the legal framework for companies of a specifically European character. Companies operating within the Community were to have the option of registering as a 'European Company', i.e. a company which is not governed by national law, but by a legal regulation established by the Community and applicable in all member states. A European Company would thus be free to operate above the legal and practical constraints stemming from the differences between the national legal systems.

Based on expert evaluations undertaken during the 1960s, the Commission in 1970 issued a Proposal for a Council Regulation on the Statute for European Companies (Kolvenbach & Hanau 1987/94, Int. Org.: 87). After discussions in the Economic and Social Committee and the European Parliament, where among other things the great diversity between the national traditions for participation was reflected, the Commission put forward a revised proposal in 1975 (CEC 1975a). Both the 1970 and 1975 proposals on European Companies contained provisions for employee participation at board level as well as through works councils. The central features, as formulated in the 1975 proposal, were as follows:

The competence of the European works councils was to be limited to matters 'which concern more than one establishment not located in the same Member State' and matters lying outside collective agreements (art. 119). Hereby, the proposal sought to avoid interfering with already existing national arrangements.

The proposal spelt out in detail the number of employee representatives to be elected in accordance with different workforce sizes and the election procedures to be applied (secret ballot among all employees). It also contained a relatively strong protection of works councillors against dismissal and discrimination, and a right to be released from work 'to the extent to which the European Works Council considers it necessary for the performance of their duties on the council' (art. 113). The operating expenses of the works council, including the expenses incurred from hiring the assistance of external experts, should be borne by the company.

As for powers *vis-à-vis* management, the proposal specified the respective areas for information, consultation and co-decision. The works council was to receive *information* at least quarterly on:

- general developments in the sectors in which the company operates;
- the business, production and marketing situation;
- the employment situation;
- production and investment programmes;

- rationalization projects;
- production and working methods, especially the introduction of new working methods;
- anything with an 'appreciable effect on the interests of the employees' (art. 120).

Further, the works council was entitled to receive the same documents, such as annual reports and annual accounts, as the shareholders.

The works council was to be *consulted* by management before decisions were taken on:

- job evaluation;
- rates of wages per job or for piecework;
- the introduction of any technical device intended to control the conduct or performance of employees;
- the whole or partial closure or transfer of an establishment;
- substantial changes of the activities of the undertaking;
- substantial organizational changes within the undertaking;
- long-term cooperation with other companies.

Consultations should be based on a report from management 'setting out and explaining the reasons for the decision [it] intends to make and the legal, economic, and social consequences that the decision is likely to have' (art. 126). If the decision would involve major changes in the activities or organization of the undertaking, and if the works council would consider employee interests to be adversely affected, the report must include a 'social plan' to be negotiated with the works council. In case of a lack of agreement between the parties, an arbitration board should settle the question. The right to negotiate on a social plan was thus framed as a genuine co-decision right.

Co-decision was also envisaged in relation to:

- rules relating to recruitment, promotion and dismissal of employees;
- implementation of vocational training;
- the fixing of terms of remuneration and methods of computing remuneration;
- health and safety measures;
- introduction and management of social facilities;
- general criteria concerning daily times of commencement and termination of work.

It is conspicuous how closely these information, consultation and co-decision rights correspond to the rules operating under the German *Betriebsverfassung* (see chapter 2). Also, it is interesting to note the similarities between the formulations on information and consultation rights in this 1975 EC proposal, and the provisions adopted in Spain five years later through the Estatuto de los Trabajadores (see chapter 4).

As for board-level representation, the proposal for a European Company Statute was again clearly inspired by the German model. It envisaged a supervisory board where one-third of the members was to be elected by shareholders, one-third by employee representatives, while the remaining one-third was to be co-opted to the board by the first two groups in common. This latter group should be 'representing general interests, possessing the necessary knowledge and experience and not [be] directly dependent on the shareholders, the employees or their respective organizations' (art. 75a).

Evidently, these proposed structures were elaborations on already existing German institutions: the principle of a one-third employee representation in force in most German companies as well as the principle of parity plus a 'neutral' representation known from the coal and steel industry. The 1975 proposal was thus a blueprint for EC industrial relations based on co-determination at the strategic level and important consultation and co-decision rights at the tactical and operational levels.

On the whole, the proposal for a European Company Statute was received positively by both industry and trade unions, although there were differing opinions on both sides, not least as to the question of employee participation. However, with the advent to power of the Thatcher government in Britain in 1979 an adoption of the proposal by the Council became unrealistic, and consequently the Council suspended its deliberations on it in 1982.

Yet, a few years later, the internal market project led to a revival of the European Company Statute. The central idea behind the plans for a specific European Company concerns the effectiveness and integration of the EC economy, while employee participation is only a side-issue in this context. It was logical to include the European Company in a project whose objective it was to remove the remaining obstacles to 'free enterprise' within the Community. So, in the 1985 White Paper on Completing the Internal Market, in which the Commission formulated the plans for the internal market in detail, the European Company was reintroduced as a policy objective (CEC 1985).

Three years later the Commission issued a memorandum on the subject (CEC 1988). Here, it once again stressed the importance of transnational European companies for the development of the EC economy as well as their ability to compete with Japanese and American enterprises. In these circumstances, a revised proposal for a European Company Statute was put forward in 1989 (CEC 1989a, b).

The early versions of the statute had the form of a *regulation* which means that it would apply directly as law in the member states. Contrary to this, the 1989 proposal was divided into a regulation with general rules for the European Company and a *directive* which contained the rules relating to employee participation. Directives do not directly have the force of law in the member states; they have to be implemented nationally, whereby a certain scope is left to the member states. The separation of the proposal into a regulation and a directive was a way by which the Commission might signal its intentions of allowing flexibility on the question of participation. Nevertheless, the text of the proposed regulation made it clear that European Companies can only be formed in member states that have implemented the corresponding directive on employee participation.

The 1989 proposal appears much diluted compared to the 1970/75 versions. First, the idea of a uniform participation system within companies registered as European had been abandoned. In the preamble it was stated that 'the great diversity of rules and practices existing in the member states as regards the manner in which employees' representatives participate in the supervision of the decisions of the governing bodies of public limited companies makes it impossible to lay down uniform rules on the involvement of employees' (CEC 1989b). Member states could now 'choose the model best corresponding to their national traditions' and companies could choose 'the model most suited to their social environment'. Yet, still the aim was to 'guarantee equivalent levels of participation and comparable influence to the employees'. With these formulations the Commission endeavoured to follow the 'subsidiarity principle' which, although unclear as to its practical implications, had been introduced as a guideline in the discussions on the internal market and its social dimension. The principle implies that the EU shall only regulate when the set objectives can be reached more effectively at the EU level than at more decentralized levels, i.e. at member state, regional or company level. Essentially, 'subsidiarity' is a flexible concept which serves as a common point of reference in the continuing discussions between 'integrationists', on the one hand, and, on the other, liberalists and nationalists, who are opposed to what they see as excessive regulation at EU level.

Secondly, the European Company Statute no longer required participation both at board level and through works councils. It now concentrated on participation only in relation to 'the supervision and strategic development' of the companies. It must be added, however, that the works councils reappeared in another draft directive aiming at transnational companies operating within the EC. This directive was issued by the Commission in 1990, also in continuation of the social dimension action programme (see below).

Thirdly, participation rights had been watered down considerably. In the 1989 proposal there was no longer any notion of parity between shareholder and employee interests at board level (just as the 1990 draft directive on works councils contained no provisions on co-decision rights).

The 1989 version of the European Company Statute operates with three different models of employee participation. A member state may restrict the choice of models or make one of the models compulsory for European Companies registering in its territory. A company registered in a given member state can choose between the models allowed in the country. The three models are:

1   At least one-third and not more than one-half of the supervisory board (in a two-tier board structure) or the administrative board (in a one-tier board structure) are appointed by the employees. This corresponds roughly to the 1976 German law on *Mitbestimmung* and is also close to the provisions in Danish company law.
2   Employees are co-opted to the board on the basis of nominations undertaken by the employee representatives (the Dutch model).
3   Employees are represented through a 'separate body'. This body has a right to be informed at least every three months on the progress of the company's business and of its prospects. It must have access to documents submitted to the general meeting, and at any time it may require information on 'any matter concerning conditions of employment'. In matters where the supervisory or administrative body has to give its authorization, the employee body is entitled to consultations with management prior to the implementation of decisions. Such matters are:

- whole or partial closures or transfers of establishments;
- substantial changes in the activities of the company;
- substantial organizational changes within the company;
- long-term and/or important cooperation with other undertakings;
- the setting up of a subsidiary or a holding company.

This third model is an accommodation to those EC countries which have no tradition of employee representation at board level.

Further flexibility is offered by allowing yet other models which may be agreed upon between management and employee representatives, though such collectively bargained models must ensure that employee representatives are given the same rights concerning information and consultation as those stipulated for the third model above. An observer close to the Commission (Venturini 1988: 52) interpreted this range of options as the possibility to choose between the German system (representation at board level), the Franco-Italian system (participation through a separate body), and the Swedish system (participation according to an agreement concluded at company level). One might add also that the British joint consultative committees, presently existing only on a voluntary basis, can fit into the proposed regulation.

The proposal requires employee representatives to be elected through a secret ballot, open to all employees, and in a way which as far as possible secures a proportional representation. The company must supply the representatives with the material and financial resources, including time off from work and the assistance of experts, necessary for enabling them to 'perform their duties in an appropriate manner'. Contrary to the 1975 proposal there are no provisions concerning protection from dismissal.

These diluted and more flexible provisions on participation did not cause UNICE to accept the proposal. It welcomed the idea of a European Company, but argued that to regulate on participation was both unnecessary and harmful to company interests (UNICE 1989). In particular, UNICE attacked the decision of the Commission to base the directive on Article 54 of the Treaty of Rome which would allow it to be adopted by a qualified majority in the Council. Opposition to the proposal was also voiced by American capital interests (Hansen 1991: 34).

From the trade union side, the ETUC on the whole expressed support for the proposal. At the same time it pointed out that the three models of the proposal were hardly equal in the influence they would give to employees, and it criticized the weakening of participation rights (ETUC 1989).

Although the Commission had scheduled the European Company Statute to enter into force as part of the internal market on 1 January 1993, the Council had still not decided upon the proposal by the end of 1994.

The drafts for a Fifth Directive

Already in the 1960s the EC Commission identified significant variations in company law across the member states as an obstacle to the development of a European common market. The national 'constitutions' for public limited companies display major differences as to how and by which categories of persons the company shall be governed. In some of the member states, e.g. Germany, companies are governed through a two-tier system consisting of a supervisory board and a management board, while other member states, e.g. Britain, have a one-tier system. In the one-tier system the board of directors/administrative board comprises persons with executive functions in the company as well as persons without such functions. Another important difference is that some countries have provisions for employee participation at board level, often in separate laws, whereas others do not. More generally, there are variations as to how responsibility and influence is divided between shareholders, managers, employee representatives and possible 'neutral' board members.

In these circumstances, and parallel to the initiatives for creating legal frameworks for a European Company, the Commission set forth a number of proposals aimed at harmonizing company law across the member states. One of these proposals was the 1972 draft Fifth Directive . . . concerning the structure of public limited companies and the powers and obligations of their organs (CEC 1972).

The proposal opted for the introduction of the two-tier system in all EC member states, arguing that this would promote the formation of transnational companies within the Community. It also called for an elimination of differences concerning worker participation 'not least because' the different rules 'constitute a barrier to the application of the Community rules which are necessary to facilitate transnational operations involving reconstruction and interpenetration of undertakings' (preamble). More specifically, the draft directive required that in companies with more than 500 employees at least one-third of the members of the supervisory board should be 'appointed by the workers or their representatives or upon proposal by the workers or their representatives' (art. 4.2). Alternatively, employee representatives should be selected by the supervisory board itself. Companies could thus choose between the German and the Dutch representation model.

The proposal was met by criticism notably from business interest organizations, but also from Britain which became a member of the EC in 1973 together with Denmark and Ireland. This led the Commission to explain its viewpoints more thoroughly in a discussion paper or green book published in 1975 (CEC 1975b). Here, it noted the board-level participation systems already in force in several of the member states and argued that this type of employee participation was beneficial to both companies and employees; a uniform regulation of participation rights was seen as essential for the economic as well as social integration of the Community:

> Too great a divergence in the laws regulating the role of employees in relation to the decision-making structures of companies constitutes not only a barrier to cross-frontier movements of companies, capital and employees, but, more fundamentally, it is also a denial of the idea of a Community as far as employees are concerned. (CEC 1975b: 10)

The advent to power in Britain in 1974 of a Labour government, committed to promoting industrial democracy, considerably improved the chances of the Fifth Directive, and it was evident that the British Bullock committee was influenced by the ideas being debated in the EC institutions at that time (Schmitthoff 1977). However, neither in Britain nor in the EC was it possible to reach the degree of consensus necessary for an actual adoption of the proposals for board-level participation (for Britain, see chapter 3). Within the EC the green book was followed by intense debates in the European Parliament and the Economic and Social Committee. Among the demands emerging from the debate were that the threshold at which the directive should apply should be raised to 2,000 employees, and that it should be made explicit that all employees should take part in the election of employee representatives to the board. This latter demand strongly contradicted the trade union representation principle especially prevalent in Britain (Kolvenbach & Hanau 1987/94, Int. Org.: 141–5).

Having attempted to take the criticisms raised into consideration, the Commission issued a revised proposal for a Fifth Directive in 1983 (CEC 1983b). The amended draft departed from the strict and comprehensive harmonization envisaged in the original proposal. It no longer required a two-tier board structure to be established, and as for participation it now allowed three different models and two different methods of implementation.

The models which member states could choose between were to be those already described in the presentation of the 1989 European Company Statute, i.e. (a) from one-third to one-half of board members are to be elected by the employees; or (b) employee representatives are co-opted to the board; or (c) employee representatives participate through a separate body. As for the implementation of the participation at board level, the revised proposal still envisaged that this would take place on the basis of legislation. But it also made it possible to introduce participation through the conclusion of a collective agreement at company level, on the condition that the representation and participation criteria of one of the three models were adhered to in the agreement. Companies were given one year to conclude an agreement; if no agreement was reached within this period employee participation should be introduced according to legislation. This again was a new approach. It was to be reiterated both in the 1989 proposal for a European Company Statute and in the 1990 proposal for European Works Councils.

Other changes in the 1983 draft Fifth Directive compared to the 1972 version were:

- employee participation was only required for companies employing more than 1,000 employees;
- participation should not be implemented if a majority of employees proved to be opposed to it;
- employee representatives should be elected according to

proportional representation systems, by secret ballot and in such a way that all employees are able to participate in the elections.

While the 1972 proposal envisaged a strict harmonization of decision-making bodies and the form of employee participation on these, it is evident that the 1983 version expressed a much more flexible approach. Member states were given the possibility, not of avoiding employee participation altogether, but of developing it along their respective industrial relations traditions. The options of creating a separate body for employee representatives and introducing participation through collective bargaining were concessions to British, Irish and Italian traditions especially.

This flexibility, however, did not make the proposal sufficiently suitable for a compromise. Political opinion in the member states had become too divergent for that. From one side, the German Minister of Labour called the proposal a 'token harmonization', and the DGB found it an 'insult' to the trade union movement and its aspirations for industrial democracy. From the other side, the British government and the CBI strongly criticized the proposal as a completely unnecessary and unwanted piece of regulation (Kolvenbach & Hanau 1987/94, Int. Org.: 148–50). At the European level the ETUC gave the proposal limited support, deploring the 'reactionary nature of the amendments', while the position of the UNICE roughly corresponded to the British attitude.

At a time when flexibility and deregulation were influential catchwords the EC Commission had tried to adapt. The 1983 draft Fifth Directive was, as already mentioned, much more flexible than the 1972 proposal. But not enough to satisfy the neo-liberalists. As for deregulation, the EC Commission did not manage to convince the employer organizations and the British government that this *one* piece of legislation would mean *less* regulation because it harmonized ten existing national pieces of regulation. To the opponents, one new piece of legislation was one too many – especially if it involved new obligations on companies which this one did in a number of member states.

Against this background, the Council abstained from taking a decision on the proposal which instead was put under consideration in a working group. When in 1990 and 1991 the Commission issued some new amendments to the draft Fifth Directive, the proposed changes were not related to the issue of employee participation. But the revisions at least confirmed that the proposal is still there. Like the European Company Statute, it has been on and off the EC agenda for more than 20 years without a final decision having been taken by the Council.

The Vredeling proposal

By the early 1970s the impact of multinational companies on economic development, national independence and social conditions was discussed intensely by governments, international organizations and trade unions (see e.g. Levinson 1972). In 1973 the EC Commission reported to the Council on the issue (CEC 1975c). The Commission found that transnational companies were posing serious problems for public authorities and workers' rights. In more precise terms, the industrial relations problem was considered as arising from the fact that regulations on employee rights in a given country have no legally binding effect for parent undertakings situated in other countries. If, for instance, a parent company in the US decides to close a subsidiary in Belgium, it is under no obligation to live up to existing Belgian rules concerning, for example, information and consultation with employee representatives prior to the implementation of the decision. Thus, multinational companies may erode the effectiveness of national regulations.

In its report the Commission specifically mentioned 'the need for appropriate representation of employees' interests *vis-à-vis* a company which no longer takes its decisions independently but complies with those of the group in which it forms part' (CEC 1975c). This problem subsequently led to the working out of a proposal for a directive on procedures for informing and consulting the employees of undertakings with complex structures, in particular transnational undertakings (CEC 1980). The proposal was issued in 1980 and was soon named the 'Vredeling Directive' after the person who at that time was Commissioner for Social Affairs.

The Vredeling proposal aimed to ensure that transnational undertakings should be subject to the same obligations towards employees, irrespective of which member state they were operating in, so that unequal treatment of employees could be prevented. The proposal put a number of demands on all parent undertakings or groups with subsidiaries with at least 100 employees in an EC member state. It included multinational firms based in Community as well as non-Community countries, and also national undertakings 'with a complex structure'.

The proposal made it mandatory for parent undertakings to disclose *information*, at least every six months, to employee representatives in subsidiaries. The information should give 'a clear picture of the activities of the dominant undertaking and its subsidiaries taken as a whole', and should relate to:

- structure and manning;
- the economic and financial situation;
- the situation and probable development of the business and of production and sales;

- the employment situation and probable trends;
- production and investment programmes;
- rationalization plans;
- manufacturing and working methods, in particular the introduction of new working methods;
- all procedures and plans liable to have a substantial effect on employees' interests (sec. II, art. 3; sec. III, art. 12).

To these information rights were added provisions for *consultations* when a decision of the parent undertaking 'is liable to have a substantial effect on the interests of the employees', i.e. in cases concerning:

- the closure or transfer of an establishment or major parts thereof;
- restrictions, extensions or substantial modifications to the activities of the undertaking;
- major modifications with regard to organization (sec. II, art. 4).

In such cases the management of the parent company must inform the management and employee representatives of the subsidiaries on:

- the grounds for the proposed decision;
- the legal, economic and social consequences of such a decision for the employees concerned;
- the measures planned in respect of these employees (sec. II, art. 4).

This information should be given 40 days before the adoption of the decision, allowing employee representatives 30 days for deliberating and giving their opinion on the proposed changes.

More intense consultations were envisaged in cases where employee representatives would regard the proposed change as 'likely to have a direct effect on the employees' terms of employment or working conditions'. Then the management of the subsidiary would be obliged to consult with them 'with a view to reaching an agreement on the measures planned in respect of them'. These formulations were reminiscent of those found in the 1975 proposal on a European Company Statute and were clearly inspired by the German provisions for the drawing up of a social plan in situations of change where employee interests are negatively affected.

The Vredeling proposal did not contain any provisions interfering with the procedures existing in the different member states as to how employee representatives should be elected. The proposal simply presupposed the existence of such representatives according to laws and customs in the individual countries. Nor did it require the creation of a body representing employees from all the eligible subsidiaries within an undertaking. It only stated that such a body might be established by agreement between the parent company and employee representatives, in which case information and consultation could take place in this forum. In other respects, however, it clearly intervened in national arrangements, the inclusion of national 'complex' companies and the right to consultations with local management being the most important examples of this.

It is obvious that the Vredeling proposal implied a number of potentially annoying restrictions for transnational and other complex companies. It required them to take employee interests into consideration and to plan major changes in an orderly and open fashion, allowing employee representatives (and local managers) the possibility of reacting before the implementation of changes. It demanded a greater degree of transparency – which is not necessarily an advantage if one of the relative strengths of multinationals is their ability to divide and rule between subsidiaries and workforces situated in different countries.

On the other hand, the Vredeling proposal was moderate compared to, for instance, German legislation on participation. There were no provisions on co-decision in the proposal, and consultations of a more intense character were confined to the level of the subsidiary. The most far-reaching clause was the one providing for consultations over measures likely to have negative consequences on employee interests. But, unlike the German *Sozialplan*, it was not backed up by a right of co-decision.

In spite of its relatively modest aims, the Vredeling proposal unleashed a storm of protest from the organizations of employers and industry and from individual multinational companies. The reaction from capital, whether based in Europe, America or Japan, was sharp and almost unanimous. Among the arguments against the proposal were that it would delay and make difficult changes within companies, reduce the competitiveness of EC countries and create an adverse relationship between employers and employees (Kolvenbach & Hanau 1987/94, Int. Org.: 57).

On the basis of the strong opposition from business organizations as well as changes proposed by the much more amenable European Parliament, the Commission published an amended proposal in 1983 (CEC 1983a). The most important changes were:

1   The directive should now only apply to complex companies with at least 1,000 workers employed in EC member states.
2   Information should only be disclosed once a year, and the demands concerning information were substantially less detailed.
3   Information on issues where employee representatives would be entitled to be heard should be given 'in good time' as against 40 days in advance in the first draft.

4   Companies were allowed not to disclose information 'which could substantially damage the undertaking's interests or lead to the failure of its plans' (art. 7.1).
5   Consultation rights were extended to include the following issues:

- major modifications in working practices or productive methods, including modifications resulting from the introduction of new technologies;
- the introduction of long-term cooperation with other undertakings or the cessation of such cooperation;
- measures relating to workers' health and safety.

All in all, the changes amounted to a considerable watering down of the original proposal. In particular, the number of companies to be affected by the directive had been reduced drastically because of the new threshold concerning workforce size. Both Commissioner Vredeling and the ETUC deplored the weakening of the proposal. The modifications, however, did not satisfy the representatives of capital, neither in Europe nor in America and Japan. American multinationals lobbied heavily in Brussels and the Japanese industrial federation, Keidanren, stated that the directive would have 'a restrictive effect on the growth of Japanese investments in Europe' (Kolvenbach & Hanau 1987/94, Int. Org.: 62).

Under these circumstances, the EC Council of Ministers could not reach a decision on the directive. The British government in particular displayed hostility towards it in principle, arguing that the question of information and consultation is best left to employers and employees themselves to decide. Finally, a Council meeting in 1986 took the directive off the agenda, referring to the problems arising from the fact that information and consultation in some of the member states are regulated solely by collective agreements (Kolvenbach & Hanau 1987/94, Int. Org.: 64). At the same time, however, the Commission was asked to go ahead with analyses of the issue and to submit an amended proposal or a new proposal in 1989.

The fate of the Vredeling proposal demonstrated with ample clarity that the times had changed. The basic ideas of the proposal were in line with public opinion and corporatist government strategies of the 1970s when it was originally conceived. By the 1980s employer organizations and the Conservative British government had united in an offensive to roll back state and trade union influence on company prerogatives. Given this situation and the requirement of a unanimous vote in the Council, the Vredeling ideas no longer had a chance.

Participation based on voluntarism?

By the mid-1980s it was evident that attempts at introducing employee participation on the basis of EC directives had reached an impasse. The employer organizations and the British government insisted that industrial relations issues should be left to a voluntaristic approach. However, there were few signs that sheer decentralist voluntarism would lead to even a minimum harmonization of participatory institutions across the member states.

The Commission, therefore, was keen to have the parties at European level – the ETUC, UNICE and CEEP – enter into discussions with a view to reaching EC-wide agreements. In 1985 the Commission sought to blow life into the *social dialogue* between the parties by initiating the Val Duchesse talks, named after a chateau near Brussels where the first discussions took place (Venturini 1988: 27). Moreover, the social dialogue was strengthened ideologically by the 1986 Single European Act which introduced into the amended Treaty an article stating: 'The Commission shall endeavour to develop the dialogue between management and labour at European level which could, if the two sides consider it desirable, lead to relations based on agreement.'

It was hoped that a closer contact between the parties might lead to solutions which at the same time could satisfy the political objectives of the 'mainstream' EC and the employers' demands for flexibility and voluntarism. If so, social dialogue could become an important alternative to the blocked legislative approach.

The Val Duchesse talks failed to meet these expectations. They resulted in the issuing of 'joint opinions' rather than binding agreements. One of the topics under discussion was information and consultation in connection with the introduction of new technologies. In a joint opinion published in 1987, both parties expressed positive attitudes towards participation practices in relation to new technology. But it was also carefully pointed out that the basis for information and consultation should be the already existing, nationally diverse, laws, agreements and practices of the different member states. No extension or harmonization of participation procedures was advocated (Venturini 1988: 95–8).

With the Maastricht Treaty and the European Union coming into force by 1 November 1993, the scope for social dialogue was further enlarged. According to the new decision-making procedures, the Commission now has to consult the labour market parties prior to deciding on new initiatives in the social area, as well as prior to the submission of a proposal to the Council. On being consulted on a proposal the parties may express a wish to regulate the issue themselves by collective agreement, thus avoiding statutory regulation. They are then given a period of nine months for negotiations and the conclusion of an agreement. If they fail to reach an agreement the Commission is free to propose a legal instrument for regulating the issue in question.

In the autumn of 1993 the UNICE proposed to the ETUC that this new social dialogue procedure should be used to work out an agreement which could serve as an alternative to the Commission proposal for a European Works Council directive (see next section). The ETUC refused the offer, however, seeing it as an opportunistic attempt on the part of the UNICE to delay further a regulation on participation in transnational companies (Munch 1993). Nevertheless, the UNICE invitation was in itself a demonstration that the social dialogue may become increasingly significant in the future. The main reason for this is not the new procedures mentioned above, but the fact that under the Treaty on European Union certain social policy proposals, for instance proposals on information and consultation, can be adopted by a qualified majority. This implies that an alliance between employer organizations and one government is no longer a safe bulwark against regulations in the industrial relations area.

Yet, the institutional strengthening of the role of the labour market organizations will hardly lead to a rapid flowering of European collective agreements. In general, the organizations lack the necessary resources, authority and internal cohesion for entering into agreements of a binding and effective character (Teague & Grahl 1992: 85). And, concerning participation in particular, there is considerable distance between the objectives of employer organizations and trade unions. On the other hand, there is no doubt that the new decision-making procedures will put particular pressure on the employer organizations. If they, together with the trade unions, cannot form the rules for European industrial relations, the politicians will do it for them. For organizations in countries with a strong tradition of voluntarism, like Britain and Denmark, this is a somewhat frightening prospect (Jensen et al. 1993).

At least theoretically, a further possibility is, of course, that industrial relations will become Europeanized on the basis of voluntarist approaches pursued within individual companies. Are there tendencies for this with employee participation? A study by Gold & Hall (1992) showed that European-level institutions for information and consultation are the exception more than the rule in European multinationals. They identified 12 multinational companies where bodies had been established or meetings had taken place between central management and employee representatives from establishments located in different countries. Most of the companies were French, and the arrangements here usually amounted to a yearly meeting for the disclosure of information and the exchange of views between central management and employee representatives; the procedures followed by and large corresponded to the rules applying to national companies under French legislation. The initiative had in most cases been taken by management. In contrast to this, in the three German companies found to have established European participation structures, the employee side had been the active party. And in at least one of the German companies, Volkswagen, a genuine right to consultation had been conceded concerning 'planned cross-border transfers of production' (Gold & Hall 1993: 12).

A later study (Carley 1993) indicated a certain extension of European-wide participation arrangements at company level, based partly on management initiatives and partly on pressure from trade unions and employee representatives. A notable growth could be seen in trade union activity. In several companies where central management did not recognize a cross-border representative body for employees, trade unions had initiated the holding of regular meetings between employee representatives from different countries. Some of these activities were supported financially by the EC Commission as a part of its promotion of social dialogue (Carley 1993: 17–18).

All in all, however, these initiatives were a far cry from a general introduction of information and consultation rights at the European level. Their importance was primarily symbolic, serving as pilot projects to demonstrate that participation structures at the transnational level, far from being a catastrophe for employers, might prove to be advantageous to both management and labour. In this way they helped to break the ground for a general regulation, as for instance the one proposed in the European Works Council directive.

The European Works Councils Directive

In the 1989 action programme related to the social charter, the Commission again argued for the need for rules on employee information and consultation within transnational companies. As the national regulation systems are ineffective in relation to decisions taken in parent undertakings located in other countries 'employees affected by decisions taken elsewhere by the parent undertaking . . . could be unequally treated', a situation which 'is bound to have a direct effect on the operation of the internal market' (CEC 1990b: 66).

Careful not to provoke the same opposition front as the one that stopped the Vredeling proposal, the Commission chose not to put forward yet another amended version of this proposal, but rather to work out a completely new proposal. The result was the 1990 draft directive on the establishment of a European Works Council in Community-scale undertakings or groups of undertakings for the purposes of informing and consulting employees (CEC 1990c).

The proposal was only directed at Community-scale companies, defined as undertakings and groups which have at least 1,000 employees within the Community, and at least two establishments with more than 100 employees in two different member states. The directive would apply to companies irrespective of whether the parent undertaking is located in an EC or a non-EC country. Such companies must establish a European Works Council as a body of representation for its employees in different workplaces/member states. The composition and functions of the works council must be negotiated between the management of the company and a special negotiating body set up by the employee representatives. Only if an agreement fails to be reached within a year, certain minimum requirements were to apply in accordance with the directive and national legislation.

Among the minimum requirements the most important ones were (CEC 1990c):

1   The European Works Council (EWC) must consist of between 3 and 30 members.
2   The EWC would be entitled to meet with the central management once a year to be informed in particular on the company's 'structure, economic and financial situation, the probable development of the business and of production and sales, the employment situation and probable trend, and investment projects'.
3   The EWC would have a right to be informed and consulted, in good time and in writing, by the central management about 'any management proposal likely to have serious consequences for the interests of the employees'; it should also be entitled to an extra meeting with management once a year in the event of such proposals arising; it was explicitly stated, however, that 'the final decision shall be exclusively the responsibility of the central management'.
4   The operating expenses of the EWC, including expenses for meeting facilities, interpretation, and travel and accommodation, must be borne by the central management of the company.

In a number of respects, the EWC proposal was both less far-reaching and more flexible than the Vredeling proposal. It was less far-reaching in the sense that it avoided interfering with existing national regulations on employee participation; the participation it suggested was strictly limited to the transnational level of companies. In this way it took into account one of the criticisms raised against the Vredeling proposal, namely that it would cut across national arrangements, for example in Germany and France where there are already provisions for group-wide employee representation (Hall 1992). The

EWC proposal was also markedly less ambitious than the works councils envisaged in the earlier versions of the European Company Statute:
instead of granting co-decision rights it emphasized management's
exclusive right to manage.

The proposal was flexible in the sense that it would be left to employers and employees to determine the exact structure, composition and
functions of the EWC – even with the possibility of agreeing *not* to set
up an EWC, provided that the minimum requirements for information
and consultation could be met by some other instrument (art. 6).
Further, it delegated to the member states the decision on how members of an EWC should be appointed.

The reactions to the proposal followed the pattern already established. The ETUC, the majority of the Economic and Social
Committee, and the European Parliament supported the proposal, but
also advocated a strengthening of employee rights in certain respects.
For instance, the majority of the Economic and Social Committee,
including the trade union group, recommended that it should be clari-
fied that the consultation right applies to such issues as 'the transfer,
concentration, cutback or closure of establishments' and 'changes in
organization or the introduction of new working methods and production processes' (Economic and Social Committee 1991). The same
attitude was expressed by the ETUC (Hall 1992: 9).

The group of employers on the Economic and Social Committee, on
the other hand, strongly criticized the proposal as a 'standardized,
stereotyped, cumbersome and bureaucratic format of employee consultation across the Community regardless of existing national and
company arrangements'. The group felt that the directive would
'inhibit companies' flexibility and speed of decision-taking' and lead to
'conflicts of interest and responsibility with established consultative
arrangements at local level'. In fact, in its argument, the employer
group seemed to express an opposition to any form of representative
participation in principle; as an alternative, the group pointed out that
'for the information and consultation to be fully effective it needs to be
direct, personal and individual' (Economic and Social Committee
1991). The reaction of UNICE (1991) was in the same vein.

By the end of 1991 the Commission issued an amended proposal,
taking into account some of the criticisms raised in the debate (CEC
1991). It followed the recommendation of the Economic and Social
Committee to include a concrete list of issues which must be considered
as having serious consequences for the employees. The definition of the
workplaces covered was changed, so that the proposal now covered
companies with at least 1,000 employees in the Community and at
least 100 employees in at least two member states; the first proposal
had required that at least 100 employees were employed in the same

establishment, thereby excluding, for instance, banks which may have more than 100 employees in one country but not in any of its individual establishments. The right of the EWC to convene prior to a meeting with the central management was stated explicitly. Finally, the level of consultations was made more flexible; instead of taking place between the EWC and the central management, the revised proposal stipulated that they could take place at some other 'appropriate' level of management.

All in all, the amendments did not change the central content of the proposal which therefore remained unacceptable to UNICE as well as the British government.

A study sponsored by the EC Commission at that time estimated that the European Works Council directive would be relevant to 880 EC-based companies employing a total of 13.6 million persons across the Community; 38 per cent of these companies had their headquarters in Britain. A further 43 companies based outside the EC, most of them in Japan and the USA, also met the criteria of the directive (Hall et al. 1993: 33).

The proposal was originally put forward under article 100 of the EEC Treaty, requiring unanimity for proposals relating to 'the rights and interests of employed persons'. In April 1993 a Council meeting resulted in all member states agreeing to the proposal in principle, except for Britain. But, as there were no signs that the British government would change its position, the Commission announced in October that it would proceed without Britain by placing the proposal under the 11-state-only procedure of the social policy Protocol and Agreement of the Maastricht Treaty (EIRR 1994a: 29). This procedure entails that management and labour at the EC level get the opportunity to make an agreement as an alternative to the legislative approach. As already mentioned, and not surprisingly, the UNICE and the ETUC were not able to agree. Consequently, by April 1994 the Commission submitted a new proposal, this time entitled: proposed council directive on the establishment of European committees or procedures in Community-scale undertakings and Community-scale groups of undertakings for the purposes of informing and consulting employees (CEC 1994).

Essentially, the contents of this proposal were identical to the latest version of the draft EWC directive. As indicated by the title, the term 'works council' had been replaced by 'committees and procedures', and, in addition, the possibility of complying with the directive through company-based voluntary agreements had been strengthened. By this, the flexibility of the possible forms of implementation was underlined. This greater scope for voluntarism was strongly criticized by the ETUC.

After yet another slightly amended proposal in early June 1994, the

11 states (with Portugal abstaining) reached agreement on a common position. Here the proposal was weakened in two respects. First, the period for negotiations to take place over a possible voluntary establishment of a European works council or a similar body was extended from two years to three. Secondly, the criteria as to which companies would be affected was changed: the overall threshold of 1,000 employees was withheld, but the demand for at least 100 employees in each of at least two member states was altered to 150 employees. The latter change somewhat reduced the number of companies to be covered by the directive. A more formal change, finally, was that 'works council' again replaced the term 'committee' (EIRR 1994a, b).

The EWC directive, including the changes mentioned above, was finally adopted at the Labour and Social Affairs Council in September 1994. At least symbolically, this marked a breakthrough for employee participation at EU level: a watered-down directive which Britain has no share in, which the employers' organizations are opposed to, and which the trade unions are not too happy with, but nevertheless the first tangible result of the long march towards bringing employee participation on a level with economic integration within the European Union.

The EWC directive has to be implemented by the member states no later than two years after its adoption. From then on employee representatives from 'Community-scale undertakings' or groups of undertakings in the member states will be entitled to start a negotiation process on the form and content of participation in these companies. If they are not able to reach an agreement with the management, they are, after three years, empowered to form a European works council. The works council will have the right to meet with the central management once a year, to be informed and consulted, on the basis of a report drawn up by the central management. The meeting may relate to the undertaking's or group's

> structure, economic and financial situation, the probable development of the business and of production and sales, the employment situation and probable trend, investment projects, and substantial changes concerning the organization, the introduction of new working methods or production processes, transfers of production, cut-backs or closures of undertakings, establishments or important parts thereof, or collective redundancies. (CEC 1994)

Further meetings are envisaged 'where there are exceptional circumstances affecting employment, more particularly in the event of relocations, the closure of establishments or undertakings or collective redundancies' (CEC 1994). Here also the works council will have a right to be informed and consulted on the basis of a report prepared by the central management. The expenses of the works council, including internal meetings before the meetings with management, will be borne by the company.

For British companies and employees the directive will lead to rather paradoxical situations. Although Britain is excluded from the provisions, some British multinationals will be covered because of the number of employees they have in the other 11 member states. Yet, employees in Britain, even if employed by those same multinationals, will not be entitled to participate in the European works councils.

Participation in relation to redundancies, company transfers and health and safety

While it has been extremely difficult for the European Commission to get through its main proposals on employee participation, some headway was made in more specific areas in the 1970s and 1980s.

In continuance of the 1974 social action programme the EC actually managed to adopt two directives granting workers' representatives a right to information and consultation on specific issues. The first was the 1975 directive on the approximation of the laws of the member states relating to collective redundancies (CEC 1975d). This directive laid down procedures for the disclosure of information and the consultation of employee representatives in the event of mass redundancies, defined as the dismissal of at least 10 employees in small establishments and at least 30 in establishments with more than 300 employees. It obliged the employer to consult with employee representatives with a view to reaching an agreement as to how the redundancies might be limited and their negative consequences for employees mitigated. The directive was amended in 1992 when the threshold was lowered to five dismissals, while the provisions on information and consultation remained essentially unchanged (CEC 1992).

The second positive result of the social action programme was the 1977 directive on the approximation of the laws of the member states relating to the safeguarding of employees' rights in the event of transfers of undertakings, businesses or parts of businesses (CEC 1977). This directive provides, in the event of a change of ownership, that the new employer must respect those collective agreements which are in force at the time of the transfer. Moreover, the directive obliges the employer to inform about the reasons for a change in ownership and its possible consequences for the employees. If changes in employment or working conditions are intended, the employer must consult with employee representatives with a view to reaching an agreement.

A third area where the EC has established common norms for employee participation is health and safety, namely through the framework directive of 1989 (CEC 1989c; Neal & Wright 1992: 15–21). This directive was a consequence of the objective of providing minimum harmonization of health and safety conditions in the workplace in connection with the creation of the internal market, an objective which the UNICE also agreed to (Tyszkiewicz 1990).

The directive obliges the employer to disclose 'all necessary information' on health and safety matters to the 'workers and/or their representatives' (art. 10). As for consultation, the directive states that employers shall 'consult workers and/or their representatives and allow them to take part in discussions on all questions relating to safety and health at work' (art. 11.1). More specifically, consultations are required in relation to the planning and introduction of new technologies regarding the health and safety consequences of the choice of equipment and changing working conditions (art. 6.3c).

The directive is silent on the structures through which employees are to be involved. It applies to workplaces without collective representatives as well as workplaces with, for instance, safety representatives, health and safety committees and works councils. Likewise, the directive is evasive regarding the actual powers granted to employees and/or their representatives; besides the right to information and consultation it stipulates a 'balanced participation in accordance with national laws and/or practices' (arts 11.1 & 11.2). This and other vague formulations reflect an attempt not to intrude in any radical way into the rather diverse decision-making structures of the member states (Vogel 1992: 49).

Despite these limitations, the directive must be seen as an important step in the long process towards Community-wide norms on employee participation. On the one hand, it went further than the predominant employer viewpoint, and the Val Duchesse social dialogue on new technologies, by actually obliging employers to consult with the employee side when new technologies are to be introduced, as well as on other issues relating to health and safety. On the other hand, it fell short of meeting the trade union demand for co-decision rights. In this way, the directive showed the contours of possible future compromises on EU-regulated participation.

Conclusions

Despite the changing economic and political climate, the European Commission has since 1970 been insistent on the need to develop structures for employee participation at the Community level. It has argued that such structures are necessary in order to (a) enhance the efficiency of the economy; (b) create equal conditions for companies as well as employees; (c) secure a certain balance between the interests of capital and labour; and (d) improve the conditions of employees through a degree of industrial democracy. In the course of time, as the pressure for radical reforms in the wake of 1968 lost ground, and as the labour movement was weakened by the impact of mass unemployment, the efficiency and equality arguments gained ascendancy over the arguments for social harmony and democracy. However, in spite of the criticisms raised by ultra-liberalism and employer organizations, the Commission stuck to its conviction that participation is beneficial for economic as well as social and political reasons. In doing so, the Commission has acted as a state power *in spe*, pursuing the objective of social integration, of classes as well as nations, within the Community.

The Commission has not been alone in attempting to promote employee participation. On the whole its initiatives have been supported by the trade union movement, the European Parliament, a majority in the Economic and Social Committee, and a majority among the member states. Yet, the constellations have shifted over time.

Roughly speaking, the first initiatives taken by the Commission aimed to generalize essential features of the German model to the whole of the EC, at that time consisting of only six countries. This became a difficult project from 1973, when Britain, Denmark and Ireland entered the EC, because of the great diversity of traditions in workforce participation among the now nine member states. So, even though attitudes towards extended participation rights were generally favourable during the 1970s, it did not prove possible to create a consensus around the type of maximum harmonization envisaged in the early versions of the European Company Statute and the Fifth Directive. There was, however, no stable or united front of opposition to the proposals. Rather, governments and national trade unions and employer organizations expressed a broad variety of concerns, concerns which were rooted mainly in the diversities of the national industrial relations systems.

This constellation changed drastically around 1980 when, on the one hand, the Vredeling proposal provoked the anger of the big and influential multinationals, and, on the other, the neo-liberalist and deregulative wave swept strongly across management as well as the British and American governments. From then on, the divisions of opinion became much clearer. While the Commission, supported by most member states and the parliament, attempted to find compromises suitable for adoption in the Council, the UNICE and the British government took a position of opposition in principle. According to them, any EC regulation on employee participation would be harmful to the economy and therefore should not be introduced. At the same time as employer organizations were uniting around this point of view, the ETUC also managed to formulate a common policy on EC-regulated employee participation, at least officially, thus overcoming the great differences in national traditions, not least between the German and British trade union movements.

Thus, the 1980s and early 1990s witnessed a Europeanization of interest articulation. While the diversity of national traditions was at the root of the various disagreements over participation in the 1970s, the debates of the 1980s rather revealed one generalized conflict. The conflict was not over the ownership or control of production, for the EC proposals no longer contained provisions for co-determination or joint decision-making. It was a class conflict, but mainly in a symbolic sense. Fundamentally, the conflict was part of a much wider struggle over the character of European capitalism. Should it be based on corporatist structures, socially responsible companies and a cooperative relationship between employers and employees? Or should it base itself on the liberalist ideas of the sovereignty of markets and managers?

Throughout the 1980s and the beginning of the 1990s, the employers were able to get their way because the British government could and would block any proposal on employee participation in the Council. It thus seemed that the decision-making structures of the EC, often referred to as creating a democratic deficit, *de facto* guaranteed the domination of capital over labour concerning industrial relations at Community level. By becoming transnational, companies could increasingly bypass the participation rights established at national level. This imbalance was actually aggravated by the passing in 1987 of the Single European Act, according to which Council decisions relating to the completion of the single market could be taken by a qualified majority, whereas decisions concerning the rights and interests of employees continued to require unanimity. Health and safety directives, though, could be adopted by a qualified majority, and for this reason it was possible in 1989 to introduce provisions on participation within this specific area.

However, the Maastricht Treaty which was adopted by the Council in December 1991, and, after many difficulties, entered into force by November 1993, changed the legislative procedures significantly. In the reformed EC, now called the European Union, industrial relations issues may be adopted by a qualified majority. One consequence of this is that Britain, or any other single country for that matter, is not able to block future decisions in this field. It further implies that the UNICE can no longer rely on its purely negative strategy. It now has to mobilize the opposition of several member states in order to avoid EU-based legislation on participation and other industrial relations issues. Or it has to take an altogether different road, namely the negotiation and conclusion of Community-wide collective agreements. This option, which until now has had little success, was strengthened by the

Maastricht Treaty. Its social policy Protocol, not signed by Britain, operates with the possibility of the EC political bodies abstaining from regulating on social issues if the 'social partners' are able to reach agreement at the European level. By introducing qualified majority voting and stimulating the conclusion of Community-wide collective agreements, the Maastricht Treaty significantly improved prospects for the development of a European industrial relations area corresponding to the increasingly transnational economy of the EU. The adoption of the directive on European Works Councils in September 1994 was the first obvious result of these procedural changes.

Future adoption of the European Company Statute, which is likely, and the Fifth Directive, which is considerably less likely, will, by and large, finish the realization of the 'participation programme' that was launched by the EC Commission in the 1970s. Figure 7.1 sketches the possible landscape of participation in the EU. It is important to add, though, that the objectives of the EU programme have been reduced considerably in the process: from elements of co-determination to relatively weak forms of consultation.

Yet, if these proposals are adopted and implemented, it will be possible to speak of a European model for employee participation: not in the way envisaged in the 1970s where the attempt was to make the German model *the* European model; but in a much more flexible and loose form, taking account of inter-European diversity while still marking a difference from the industrial relations regimes predominant in the US, Japan and elsewhere in the world. It will be a somewhat blurred model which, regarding employee participation, will place the EU in an intermediate position between the two contesting types of capitalism described by Albert (1993) as the American model and the Rhine model.

If, on the other hand, participation is not consolidated at the EU level, national participation models would slowly but surely be eroded, as the character of the EU economy becomes increasingly supranational. Europe would then move in the direction of the American model characterized by a low degree of collective employee influence.

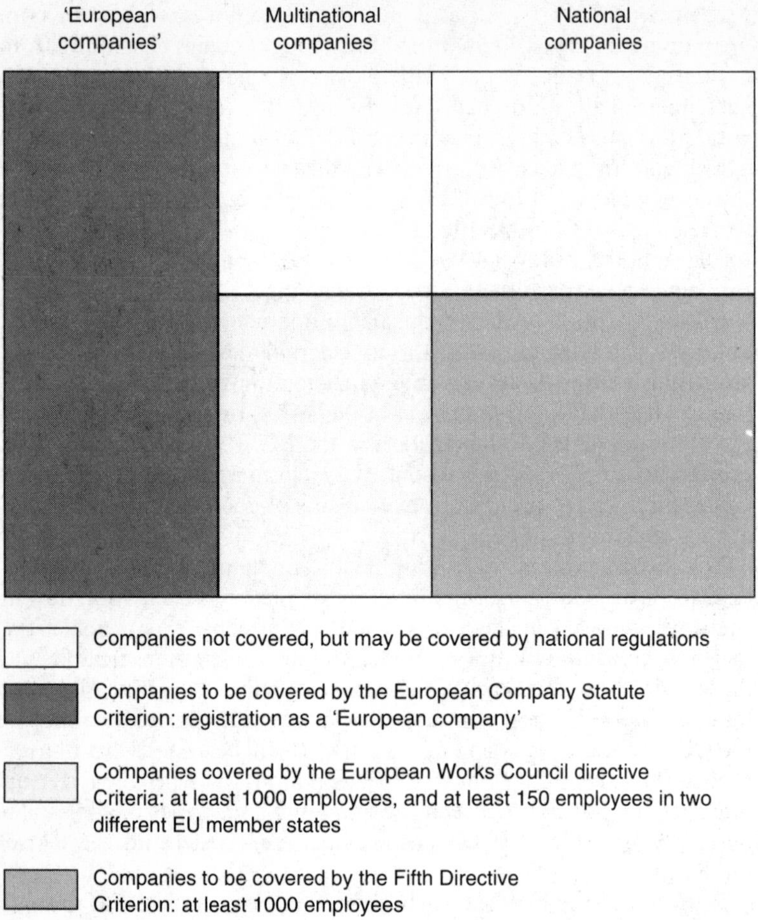

Additionally, all companies are covered by the directive on company transfers, and, except for very small ones, the directives on redundancies and on health and safety.

Figure 7.1 *Coverage of possible EU directives on participation*

8

New Technology: a Compelling Reason for More Participation?

In chapter 7 we saw that so far political initiatives at the European Community level have only led to a limited degree of convergence. It was also indicated that multinational companies only seldom establish supranational participation structures on their own initiative.

In this chapter we will continue the search for possible factors creating convergence by focusing on the impact of new technology on employee participation. There is a long tradition of regarding technology as a dynamic and revolutionizing force in society and working life (see e.g. Blauner 1964; Marx 1973; Mallet 1975). Furthermore, in two of the theories concerning convergence presented in chapter 1, technology plays an important role. In Marxist theory, technology, or 'the forces of production', is seen as the driving force for social change, and therefore also for a possible convergence between social forms. Similarly, the convergence thesis put forward by Kerr takes as its point of departure 'industrial society' which is essentially defined by its production technology.

In these circumstances, I find it relevant to raise and confront the following questions: have the changes in production, administration, planning and communication caused by the widespread application of information technology during the past two decades led to systematic changes in employee participation? Is information technology a factor which requires definite forms and a definite intensity of employee participation in order to function in an optimal way? And does information technology therefore function as a converging factor tending to break down traditional national differences in participation patterns?

In the country profiles of chapters 2–5 we have already seen that new technology has had some consequences for employee participation. In all the countries studied, new technology seems to have contributed to an increase in different forms of direct participation, such as autonomous groups, quality circles and project groups. As for indirect participation, Denmark and Germany in particular showed examples of representative bodies gaining a more active role in connection with technological changes. Yet, it was also demonstrated that only in Denmark has the technology issue led to changes in national provisions concerning participation (the 1981 Technology Agreement, later incorporated into the Cooperation Agreement).

All in all, these observations from individual countries are rather inconclusive in relation to the questions raised above. In this chapter a more global approach is applied; perhaps this will produce clearer results.

Participation as a productive necessity?

When it became evident that technologies based on micro-electronics would penetrate working life profoundly there were many predictions of revolutionary effects: it was thought that fundamental dimensions such as the demand for labour power, the localization of work, the skills needed in work, the control over work, and the very content of work, would be affected in dramatic ways. There were optimists as well as pessimists, determinists as well as voluntarists. Today, it is possible to see that many predictions shot far past the goal. It is also possible to evaluate on the basis of empirical evidence rather than an unknown future.

Among the theories of the 1970s, some were rather pessimistic concerning the impact of information technology on work and employee influence over work. Braverman (1974) saw the potential of information technology for making the Taylorist management style and work organization complete; he stressed the technical possibilities for increasing hierarchical control and the subdivision of work tasks, thus diminishing the skills and discretion needed by the worker.

The pessimistic prediction of Braverman proved to be wrong, at least as a general trend. A lot of research from the 1980s, the most influential being the study by Kern & Schumann (1985), pointed to the fact that, particularly in the advanced sectors of industry and service, a Taylorist approach fails to reap the full potential of information technology. It was found that an optimal use of the new tools and systems required the workers to have increased skill levels, to be able to exert a greater degree of discretion, and to be responsible and motivated. In this situation employee participation, which earlier was advocated mainly by the trade union movement and social–liberal reformers at government level, increasingly became interesting for managers, in its capacity as a productive force (Fröhlich et al. 1991: 51). Some observers, for instance Rojot (1986: 196) went so far as to proclaim participation as a productive necessity: 'management cannot simply demand co-operation and initiative, as opposed to a simple level of performance of simple tasks. Co-operation and initiative must be voluntary. Therefore, the use of participative management in areas such as job enrichment, quality circles, participation in decision-making, etc. is also mandatory.'

The thesis of participation as a productive necessity is rooted in the notion that a shift has occurred, or is occurring, from the mass-production paradigm of Fordism to a new era characterized by a number of different but related concepts, such as post-Fordism, new production concepts, and flexible specialization (Elam 1990). A central feature of post-Fordism is that it aims at more flexible and more differentiated forms of production and service. Because of the potential for flexibility inherent in information technology, but also because of other factors such as rapidly changing markets, the rising demand for more customized products and services and the growing uncertainty associated with both market and technological options, Taylorist mass production is on the retreat while more flexible forms of production are advancing. For this shift to be successful, the motivation and commitment of employees have to be enhanced, and participation is advocated as one of the possible instruments for accomplishing this.

The great attention paid to human resource management since the early 1980s has been interpreted as a confirmation and a logical consequence of these tendencies. Changing business conditions put a premium on those companies which develop and motivate their workforce. However, as pointed out by Storey & Sisson (1993), human resource management seems to be more ideology than reality. Moreover, it does not necessarily include employee participation, and particularly not representative forms of participation.

More generally, it is debatable to what extent a shift away from Taylorism and Fordism has taken place and what the consequences for employee participation are. Some researchers have stressed that the changes are much more gradual and much less radical than those indicated by Kern & Schumann (1985) and Piore & Sabel (1984) (see e.g. Hyman 1990; Altmann 1992b). In all events, when it comes to the more specific relation between new technology and participation it seems that, not just the overall production paradigm, but also a number of more mundane factors are at play. Deery (1992) has found that the degree of participation is connected with:

1   *Management's technological objectives and dependency on labour.* New technology may be introduced for a variety of reasons: improvement of product quality, savings in manpower or raw materials, improvement of information and control etc. It is only for some of these objectives that the skills, motivation and cooperation, and therefore participation, of the workforce is essential.
2   *Pre-existing management styles.* If the relations between management and labour are based on a tradition of cooperation and trust, it is likely that management will seek to involve the employees in the process of change. If on the contrary relations are marked by

conflict and adversarial attitudes, management will typically attempt to decide unilaterally.

3   *The type of innovations introduced.* Participation is more likely when changes are of a piecemeal, incremental character than when they involve a radical or major change of the whole or central parts of the production process.

4   *Trade union power.* Finally, participation is found to be positively correlated with trade union presence and strength in the workplace.

These factors point to the fact that the relation between information technology and participation is to a large degree of a non-determinist character. To speak of a productive necessity for participation seems an over-generalization which will place us in the opposite situation of the one predicted by Braverman. Information technology, after all, does not by itself promote or reduce the participation of employee representatives in decision-making. Social actors, notably employers and managers on the one side, and trade unions and employees on the other, are the ones who determine, within given technological as well as social environments, how technology is chosen, introduced and used in the workplace. Do these actors act in uniform ways, across geographical and cultural frontiers? We shall first turn to these social actors at the level of interest organizations, and thereafter at workplace level.

Trade unions: high expectations

The first reactions of European trade unions to information technology were of a defensive character. Trade unions emphasized the protection of jobs and of trade or skill demarcations. This was a traditional response not unlike the one developed earlier towards other types of technology. The overall decisions and criteria concerning technology were accepted as a management prerogative, whereas the consequences of these decisions for employment and skill requirements were turned into negotiation issues. In some areas, such as the printing industry, this approach proved to be totally inadequate. When management had prepared the introduction of technologies which simply made whole categories of skilled workers superfluous, there was not much to negotiate about. Bitter confrontations ensued and almost inevitably ended in defeat for the trade unions.

This kind of experience gave rise to attempts to develop more offensive and proactive strategies within the trade union movement. Instead of just focusing on the implementation and use of technology, trade unions began to direct their attention to the earlier stages of the process of change, to the way in which technology was introduced, and to the planning phase where choices are made between alternative technological solutions. The goal, at least for the more 'modern' trade unions, became to negotiate change rather than negotiate on the consequences of change.

These heightened ambitions were reflected in the programmes of national trade union organizations as well as in the policies adopted by the ETUC, the European Trade Union Confederation. At its congress in Stockholm in 1988, the ETUC demanded (Fröhlich et al. 1991: 31–2):

- the right of employee representatives to be fully informed, consulted and also to negotiate on all important company matters before decisions are taken;
- equal participation by employee representatives in all company decisions of significance to the workforce;
- extension of decision rights at all levels of decision-making according to the organization of companies (i.e. in multinational companies).

The preferred method for achieving influence was the negotiation of specific technology agreements (Gill 1985: 117–41). The British TUC, for instance, in 1979 decided that unions should attempt to negotiate agreements which included the following elements: *procedural* rights on consultations prior to equipment purchase, effective bargaining machinery on technical change, disclosure of relevant information in good time, and joint review and study teams to monitor the effects. These procedures should be coupled with attempts to gain *substantive* concessions in relation to employment and output, training, reduced working week, equipment design, and health and safety (Beirne & Ramsay 1992a: 39). In Denmark, the central technology agreement concluded in 1979 between the trade union confederation and the employers' association granted employee representatives a right to information and consultation. In Germany, the trade unions aimed at comprehensive agreements regulating the conditions of work and labour performance according to ideas of a 'human design of work' (Altmann 1992a: 381).

The basic idea concerning technology agreements was that these should bring the trade union movement into a more active position in relation to information technology; they should not only defend existing employment and working conditions, but also give trade unions and employee representatives a significant influence over the design of technology, jobs and skill profiles. A proactive trade unionism was knocking on the door – but it did not get in.

Employers: consultation yes, co-decision no

Employers and their organizations in Western Europe have also taken a positive position towards the involvement and participation of employees in technical change at the workplace. However, in general, they have not been interested in the forms of participation wanted by the trade unions. Employer organizations, as well as the great majority of companies, have refused to concede any negotiation or co-determination rights to trade unions or employee representatives in works councils and similar bodies. Their line has been to inform the elected representatives and maybe to consult them, but still preserve the right to manage as an undivided function of ownership. At the same time, employers have taken a greater interest in the direct participation of individual employees or groups of employees. Voluntary consultations with workforce representatives combined with the direct involvement of employees are seen as the best way to reap the productive rewards of new technology, without jeopardizing the right to manage and control over the labour process.

As shown in chapter 7, the European employers' association (UNICE) is strongly opposed to any ideas of statutory regulation at the EU level concerning employee participation. Instead the UNICE has opted for the subsidiarity principle and status quo: 'Such matters [i.e. participation] must be worked out by the parties most directly concerned, according to local conditions, traditions and legislation. In this way, the solutions arrived at will be better, and the parties will be more deeply committed to making them work' (quoted from Fröhlich et al. 1991: 32).

Within a framework created by the EC Commission, the ETUC and UNICE met from 1985 to 1987 to discuss employee participation in relation to the introduction of information technology. The result of these talks (the Val Duchesse talks) only amounted to a declaration of intent, a Joint Opinion in EC language. Here, it was stated that when technological change of major consequence for the workforce is introduced, workers and/or their representatives should be informed and consulted in accordance with the laws, agreements and practices valid in the Community countries, 'the final decision being exclusively the responsibility of the employer or of the decision-making bodies of the firm', which again 'does not exclude the possibility of negotiation where the parties take a decision to that effect' (quoted from Fröhlich et al. 1991: 35).

The content of the Val Duchesse Joint Opinion reflects the viewpoints of 'enlightened' managers. Although it refers to national practices (thereby also endorsing practices of no participation whatsoever) it generally stresses the importance of information and consultation. This may be interpreted as a limited concession to the trade unions. However, measured against the ETUC's much more far-reaching demands for negotiation and co-determination rights, and its wishes for a binding agreement, Val Duchesse did not give any concessions: participation yes, but without infringing on the decision-making rights of the employers.

Experience at workplace level

Within the EU countries numerous case studies have thrown light on the question of employee participation in relation to the introduction of new technology at company or workplace level (see e.g. Hyman & Streeck 1988; Altmann et al. 1992; Beirne & Ramsay 1992a; Clausen et al. 1992). The case studies are useful as qualitative evidence of the different forms and intensities of participation which have been practised, and they certainly expose a wide spectrum, ranging from intensive co-determination through all the different stages of technological innovation to no employee participation at all. In general, the case studies, as well as some national surveys, seem to confirm the conclusions drawn by Deery (1992), namely that the degree of participation is related to factors such as the specific character of the technological objectives and their dependency on the workforce (e.g. Fröhlich et al. 1989; Jones 1989; Regini 1992), management style (e.g. Price 1988) and trade union power (e.g. Daniel 1987; Müller-Jentsch & Sperling 1992).

The frequent contention that the *direct* involvement of workers and other employees is an alternative to the *indirect* participation through elected representatives is on the whole not confirmed by research. For instance Daniel (1987) found that consultations with individual employees were more common in unionized than in non-unionized firms. As to the democratization inherent in direct employee involvement, Beirne and Ramsay (1992b) reached rather disappointing conclusions. In a study on employee involvement in the design and application of computer systems, they found that user involvement one-sidedly tended to reflect employer interests, and hardly ever consciously aimed to meet employee interests and improve working conditions.

Altmann (1992b) focuses especially on the consequences of what may be termed the 'organizational–technical revolution' (Müller 1991) made possible by information technology. He stresses the integrating and pervasive potentials of information technology and tendencies towards 'systemic rationalization'. Through concepts such as CIM (computer integrated manufacturing) not only all in-plant processes are integrated, but also supply and distribution processes which take place outside the company (for example with the aim of securing just-in-time production). Flexibility is sought primarily through technology, not manpower, and employee participation does certainly not appear to be a necessity. This type of integration, according to Altmann, actually weakens the possibilities for employee representatives to exert influence, partly because decisions are taken at places other than where the effects appear, and partly because the representatives do not have the resources necessary for assessing the consequences of such comprehensive change. These tendencies are being further sharpened as technological integration is increasingly taking place across industries and on an international level.

In a review of European case studies, Cressey (1992) found that trade unions on the whole have failed to achieve the kind of technology agreements they have been advocating. This has partly been due to employer resistance, but also to the fact that binding agreements are difficult to reach because technical innovation places both parties in a situation marked by uncertainty. Proactive types of involvement have also been rare, reflecting among other things unions' fear of losing their identity and becoming 'co-managers', and their lack of resources and expertise.

The only comparative study which covers all EC countries is the survey carried out by the European Foundation in the years 1987–88 (Fröhlich et al. 1991). The aim of the study was to measure the opinions of managers and employee representatives who were involved in the introduction of new technology of a type which could be defined as having a significant impact in the workplace. Some 7,326 persons (covering 2,807 companies) were interviewed, half of them being managers, the other half employee representatives. The sample was confined to establishments with at least 50 employees and with formal institutions for employee representation, and furthermore to establishments which claimed to involve the representatives in processes of technological change. These criteria mean that the results presented below systematically overestimate the extent of employee participation in European workplaces.

Figure 8.1 shows the degree to which employee representatives (shop stewards, works councillors or other types of representative) were involved in decisions concerning new technology in the planning and implementation phase respectively. It is surprising, given the criteria for the selection of the survey sample, that a significant percentage was not involved at all. Further, it is evident that participation was both more intensive and more frequent in relation to the implementation than to the planning of new technology. Less than a quarter of the representatives were in contact with management concerning planning, while 39 per cent were so in relation to implementation. Finally, it can be seen

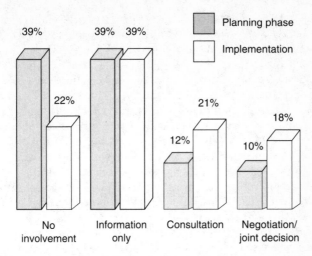

Fig. 8.1   *Intensity of participation in planning and implementation of new technology: all EC countries (European Foundation 1990)*

that the methods of participation preferred by employer organizations, information and/or consultation, were put into practice in a majority of cases, whereas the preferred methods of the trade unions, negotiation or joint regulation (co-determination), were applied only in a minor fraction of the cases.

Both employee representatives and managers expected the intensity of participation to increase in the future; negotiations or joint decision-making was expected by 17 per cent of managers for the planning phase, and by 29 per cent for the implementation phase. The corresponding figures for employee representatives, however, were 40 and 47 per cent. Among employees, a large majority expected either joint deci-sion-making/negotiation or consultation, while the emphasis among managers was on consultation or information only. This may point to future conflicts around decisions concerning information technology; at least one must expect that the commitment of employees, so often stressed as an important feature of technological innovation, will be rather limited in those workplaces where the participation expecta-tions of the employee side are frustrated by management.

In assessing the effects of participation, very few employee represen-tatives as well as managers reported negative effects. Among managers, more than one-third found that participation improves the quality of decisions and the identification of the workforce with the goals of the enterprise, and more than half stated that it facilitates the utilization of skills and increases the acceptance of new technology among employees.

The highest rate of negative effects was reported in relation to questions concerning the time needed for decision-making and implementation of the technology. But even here only about 10 per cent of managers found that participation increased the time needed, whereas around 25 per cent indicated that participation actually reduced the time needed. Even where participation took place in the form of negotiations or joint regulation, managers who found positive time effects outnumbered those finding negative ones, with a majority reporting no effects at all (Fröhlich et al. 1991: 100). The frequently voiced employer objection to joint regulation/co-decision, that it delays important decisions and slows down the process of change, was thus not confirmed.

Overall, the more intensive the participation had been, the more often positive effects were reported. For instance, where participation had been limited to information, about 50 per cent of managers reported positive effects on workforce acceptance of the technology, whereas, where the participation had taken the form of joint decision-making or negotiations, as many as 70 per cent recorded positive effects. In relation to certain other issues, such as the utilization of skills, managers saw consultation as the most effective type of participation (Fröhlich et al. 1991: 98–111).

The European Foundation study also included a comparison between the different EC countries of the intensity of employee participation in relation to technological change. Figure 8.2 shows the different forms of participation applied in the implementation phase, according to managers. Figure 8.2 demonstrates a clear north–south divide within the EC. Except for Greece, the southern European countries, including France, have markedly weaker forms of participation than the countries in the north. If we look at the strongest form of participation, negotiations or joint regulation, Denmark and Germany come out on top. Consultations are most frequently found in the United Kingdom, Ireland, the Netherlands, Belgium and Greece.

Responses from employee representatives on the whole gave a similar picture as far as the rank order between the countries is concerned. Yet, on average, they reported a somewhat lower involvement: 33 per cent reported consultation or negotiation/joint decision-making to have taken place as against 39 per cent among managers (Fröhlich et al. 1991: 68).

The above data concern the implementation phase. As to the planning phase, according to managers as well as employee representatives, the extent of participation was also highest in Denmark and Germany. This confirms the conclusions drawn earlier in this book concerning the spread of proactive types of participation in these countries.

Inspired by Deery (1989) Fröhlich et al. developed an explanatory framework for understanding the differences between EC countries

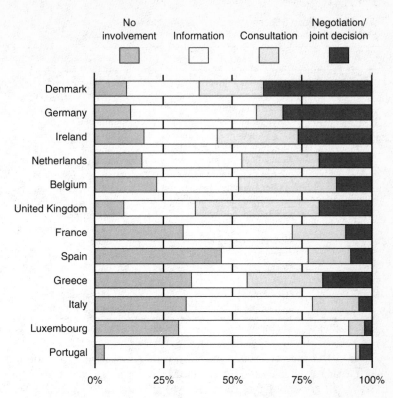

Fig. 8.2 *Intensity of participation in implementation of technology in EC countries (European Foundation 1990)*

observed in the survey (see table 8.1). The authors concluded that the explanatory factors – technological objectives, management style, bargaining power, regulation, and industrial relations system – could explain a substantial part of the variations between the countries. They also stressed that the national participation profiles are products 'of the way the contours of each Member State's industrial relations system have been shaped by wider political, economic, social and historical forces' (Fröhlich et al. 1991: 288). The European Foundation study thus confirms the conclusion drawn in chapter 6 of this book, namely that national industrial relations structures and traditions (including regulation and bargaining patterns) significantly affect the extent and intensity of participation. Here we can add that technological objectives and management style play a role, too. But these factors are hardly completely independent of industrial relations; to some extent they reflect what is possible and normal within a given industrial relations system.

Table 8.1   *Factors affecting employee participation in technological change*

Variable	Favourable conditions	Unfavourable conditions
Technological objectives	Performance enhancement and problem-solving skills important for success	Cost reduction with little dependence on employees
Management style	Cooperative	Conflictual and closed
Bargaining power	Highly unionized; facing common technological threat, and strategically located; technically knowledgeable and skilled membership; united and cohesive union organization	Multi-unionism, low unionization, facing uncertain or variable impact from technology; lack of research resources; inexperienced officials; unions divided along political or religious lines
Regulation	Established traditions of tripartite corporatism; strong forms of law	'Voluntaristic' 'market forces' or weak forms of legislation
Industrial relations system	Centralized collective bargaining agreements	Decentralized collective bargaining agreements

Source: Fröhlich et al. 1991: 148

What the European Foundation study does not confirm is the notion that information technology necessitates employee participation. The great variations among the countries testify to this, and so does the fact that a large proportion of the companies included in the study had introduced new technology without the participation of employee representatives. Furthermore, it must be remembered that the survey sample was biased in favour of companies with a participatory management style.

Towards new forms of social exchange

From the material presented briefly in the preceding sections, it seems evident that companies have much to win by increasing employee participation in relation to technological change. In a wider perspective, market pressures which put a premium on technological innovations should make us question the adequacy of existing regimes and modes of regulation at workplace level. In environments marked by rapid change and increasing uncertainty as to the market and technological options of tomorrow, workplace regimes based on a top–bottom approach to decision-making, and a more or less adversarial type of collective bargaining, are unable to produce optimal innovations and adaptations. Such regimes foster employees who conceive of the employment relation as essentially an exchange of obligations and rights. On the one hand, the obligation to work under the direction of the employer; on the other, the right to a certain pay and protection against hazards at work, unfair dismissal, etc. In this equation work itself is on the negative side while notably the financial remuneration constitutes the positive side. Furthermore, employment is seen as a static rather than a dynamic relationship.

The challenge for management in relation to technological innovation and uncertainty is not to remove this form of exchange – for a transparent and institutionally secured employment contract with its rights and obligations is an indispensable basis. Without it there would not be the job security necessary for the development of relations of trust and long-term commitments. The real challenge is how to supplement the 'classical' form of exchange with additional exchanges based on notions of plus-sums to be developed and enjoyed by both parties, and making dynamic adjustments possible. By offering training, involvement in decision-making, more interesting work, and professional and personal development through work, managers can begin to change the instrumental and restrictive employee attitudes which are the consequences of the pure work–pay exchange. Within such an approach, work will increasingly lose its meaning as a mere obligation; it becomes easier for employees to experience work as a means of human as well as productive development, and their motivation, commitment and sense of responsibility are consequently increased.

In northern Europe, and especially in Denmark and Germany, at least a visible fraction of establishments has embarked upon this venture. This has happened in spite of the evident obstacles to these new forms of exchange. For employers, a shift to greater employee involvement questions the traditional borderline between management and labour as well as the existing hierarchy in the organization. For unions and employee representatives, it is a problem that they have limited experience and knowledge of technological options at the tactical level. Moreover, it is a difficult calculation to weigh the influence gained through participation against other forms of influence which they may be restrained from using. A participative influence and consent at the tactical level as to the selection and shaping of technological solutions make it more difficult for them to protest or negotiate over the possible negative consequences of these solutions appearing later at the operational level. As noted by Clausen and Lorentzen (1993: 28) employee representatives often find themselves in a dilemma between participative/offensive and traditional/defensive forms of interest representation:

> On the one hand . . . it is already possible to find the shop stewards' 'fingerprints' on management's innovation plans . . . On the other hand, the shop

stewards' increasing involvement in questions of the daily running of the enterprise, and management's desire to see them as 'ambassadors' among the employees, implies a shift from a more traditional role of taking care of collective interests to a role of also participating in the company's development. This change may also imply a risk of becoming the management's 'hostage', without real influence when seen from the perspective of collective interests.

This dilemma can hardly be overcome. But it can be handled in tolerable ways within industrial relations systems characterized by a high level of trust and by an institutionally secured balance of power which is favourable to employee interests. Germany is a case in point. Here, the laws on works councils and co-determination secure the employees relatively strong institutional rights on the basis of which a tradition of cooperative workplace relations has developed. Müller-Jentsch et al. (1992) have pointed out that technological change and rationalizations in Germany have led to what they call informal 'modernization contracts' between management, works councils and employees. Through a set of exchanges between the two parties, management seeks to ensure that, when new technology is introduced, it happens without challenging the interests of employees. The contract may include a proactive involvement of employees and employee representatives, but usually it does not; first of all it aims to make sure that technological change takes place without dismissals, deskilling and wage reduction, and in observance of protective legislation. In return, management can expect the employees to accept and work positively for the modernization processes within the workplace. As mentioned in chapter 2, there are also examples of employee representatives playing an active role in relation to, for example, training opportunities and work organization. Similar arrangements, sometimes including more proactive types of trade union and/or employee involvement, can be found in the Scandinavian countries (Cressey 1992; Müller-Jentsch & Sperling 1992).

It thus seems that, among our four countries, the German and the Danish models in particular allow participation to be rooted as an important mode of regulation in relation to technological innovation. In other national systems where the institutional safeguards of employee interests are much weaker, it is a bigger risk for employee representatives as well as managers to depart from the traditional modes of regulation.

So, what we find is not a convergence of the forms of employee participation through technological development. Rather it is the case that specific technological strategies are best practised within specific industrial relations cultures. Indeed, seen in a wider perspective, this could be a factor aggravating the existing diversity between EU countries. Put crudely: technologies 'suited to' participatory management will be developed and applied in countries with well-established traditions of employee participation, whereas technologies 'suited to' a unilateral management style will be placed in countries with no such tradition.

Conclusions

The widespread application of information technology during the past two decades has not been accompanied by radical changes in employee participation patterns, and in general there is no empirical basis for the contention that new technology has made participation a productive necessity. Although the need to involve and motivate employees in order to reap the full benefits of information technology is well documented, it is also evident that information technology may be introduced and used successfully in accordance with authoritarian and/or Taylorist management styles. Whether information technology will lead to increased participation depends on a number of factors of which the objective of a particular technological change, management style and industrial relations tradition at national and company level are the most important.

This non-deterministic conclusion does not imply that information technology has had no repercussions for employee participation; it has indeed, but the repercussions vary from company to company, and from country to country. On a general level, information technology, because of its productive potential and the new role it gives to human labour, has led to an increased interest in employee participation, and numerous companies have been active in developing new forms of participation. It is beyond doubt that for many types of work the successful implementation and utilization of information technology is dependent on the good will and motivation of the workforce. This tends to favour increased direct participation, and possibly also increased indirect participation.

At the same time, it seems obvious that the full potential of participation is not being exploited. Although several positive effects of participation are well known to them, many managers miss the opportunity to involve their employees in decisions concerning technology. Some trade unions and employee representatives have reservations, too. Especially in countries with a tradition of adversarial industrial relations, such as Spain and Britain, they may be sceptical towards entering into participation in decisions at the tactical level, owing to a fear of becoming responsible for management decisions. Even within a cooperative industrial relations culture there are several obstacles to participation in decisions at the tactical level. Employee representatives often lack the resources and expertise necessary for intervening in those processes in which technologies are developed or selected and jobs are designed. Particularly when technological change aims to integrate processes across company and national borders, employee representatives and trade unions are poorly equipped to match the plans of management. All in all, actual participation lags behind its potential both as a productive and as a democratic force.

Compared to what one would expect from the post-Fordist literature, the average extent and intensity of participation in the EU countries is relatively low. The negotiations and co-decisions demanded by the trade union movement are rarely practised forms of participation, in spite of the fact that those managers who have tried find the effects overwhelmingly positive. Even the consultations and information disclosure advocated by employers' organizations are far from being applied universally.

The survey conducted by the European Foundation revealed wide variations across the EC member states as to the extent and intensity of technology-related employee participation. Although the results cannot be used to reject completely the idea that global technologies act as a converging factor on social forms, they certainly do not lend support to technology as a strong factor for the promotion of convergence between nationally different participation patterns. The combination of a wide range of global technological options on the one side, and diverse industrial relations systems on the other, may just as well point to a sharpening of national diversities as companies will tend to locate a given technology in those environments they find best suited for its successful implementation and use.

9

Conclusions and Perspectives

Employee participation in management decisions is neither a universal nor a uniform phenomenon. The contents of this book demonstrate that, even within a relatively small and culturally homogeneous part of the world such as the European Union, there are significant differences between countries. In Germany and Denmark employee participation has become an essential mode of regulation within the typical workplace regime; here, participation is situated within industrial relations systems where compromises, cooperation, and a certain degree of sharing of power, are central values. Contrary to this, participation is, in general, not a rooted feature of Spanish and British workplace relations; in these countries industrial relations are to a large extent interpreted as adversarial. This leaves little room for relations based on trust and notions of common interests without which participation cannot become consolidated.

Of course, these generalizations should not be taken too far. One exception that must be mentioned is the not inconsiderable share of British companies which have established a participatory workplace culture. And as for Denmark, Spain and Germany it appears that there are great differences within each country concerning whether and how the national provisions are applied in practice. The important thing to stress in this context, however, is that existing participation patterns are to a large extent embedded in institutions which are reflections of historical class compromises at the national level. The process of institutionalization has been strongest in Germany, and weakest in Britain.

In spite of significant national diversities, it is possible to detect common cyclical development trends for these four EU countries, with Spain as a partial exception. Worker participation was put on the agenda in the years following the two world wars and in the late 1960s and early 1970s, i.e. in periods when the labour movement was on the offensive and, to varying degrees, was able to challenge the existing social order. The great majority of the formal institutions for employee participation in force in the EU member states date from the latter part of the 1940s and the 1970s. Fundamentally, they must be understood as political accommodations to the labour movement's aspirations for industrial democracy – accommodations accomplished by the state in order to promote the integration of the working class in society.

Since the end of the 1970s, mass unemployment, the relocation of industry, and political–ideological conjunctures, have placed the labour movement in a relatively weak position. At the same time employer organizations have raised an opposition in principle to the development of representative or indirect forms of participation. In this, they appear to have been guided more by the predominant ideological current and traditional class instinct than by the actual experience of managers. The policies pursued by the UNICE and other employer organizations obviously contradict the positive experiences concerning participation reported by managers in several studies, notably the comprehensive survey carried out by the European Foundation.

In these circumstances, the last 15 years have witnessed an almost complete standstill in the development of representative employee participation. This goes for the four countries studied in this book as well as for most other EU countries and the EU itself. Partly because of the balances of power nationally, and partly because of the blocked initiatives at the European Community level, the 1980s and early 1990s saw a virtual freeze on representative forms of participation. The world changed, Europe changed, but collective workforce participation did not. Yet, below this main trend there were other trends at work, actually changing participation or preparing for changes at a later stage.

First, although the evidence is limited, it seems obvious that there has been an increase since the 1970s in direct forms of participation. This development has taken place at company level and almost exclusively at the initiative of management. As part of the drive for human resource management it has been motivated, not by concerns for industrial democracy or social integration at the societal level, but for greater efficiency, flexibility and quality in technologically sophisticated work. Thus, in accordance with the demands for more flexibility and deregulation, the initiative has to a considerable degree shifted from trade unions and governments to the managers in individual companies. At the same time, the discourse on employee participation has increasingly emphasized production needs rather than social or human needs. However, there is no strong evidence indicating that direct forms of participation have aimed at replacing or weakening indirect participation and trade union influence, as is often the case in American management strategies. Examples from Germany and Denmark in particular have shown that direct and representative participation may co-exist and even mutually reinforce each other.

Yet, there is hardly any doubt that trade unions and institutions such as works councils are affected in profound ways by management initiatives aimed at increasing the involvement of the individual worker.

Evidence from Britain in particular suggests that human resource strategies favour a moderate and cooperative trade unionism at the expense of more militant organizations. More generally, the greater stress put on human resources and different forms of direct participation constitute a considerable challenge to collective labour organizations. Trade unions and works councils need to develop new resources and tactics in order to gain influence on this terrain, and to prevent new forms of exchange from undermining important employee rights.

Secondly, participation has remained a European political issue. The European Commission, the ETUC and the European Parliament have insisted that some kind of institutionalized participation shall apply to all (large) companies operating within the European Community. The proposals from the 1970s which, roughly speaking, sought to generalize the German model to the entire EC, have been diluted, so that the formula now is consultation rather than co-decision. This implies that they can no longer be interpreted as fundamental threats to management prerogatives (although this is still the position of the UNICE). With the new decision-making procedures in the European Union it now finally seems that the stalemate can be broken. In this respect, the adoption in September 1994 of the directive on information and consultation in multinational companies represented an important breakthrough.

In chapter 1, I argued that a variety of theories from the social sciences lend support to the expectation that a convergence will occur between social institutions, including institutions for employee participation within the European Community. Has such a convergence taken place? Will it take place in the future?

At first sight it is tempting to conclude that all theories have failed – that no convergence has appeared. The economies of the nation states have increasingly been internationalized and integrated within the EU, and politically a wide range of decisions has been transferred from the national capitals to Brussels. But, as far as institutions for employee participation are concerned, hardly anything has happened. Nor can it be confirmed that technology has acted as a strong lever for extended and more uniform participation, at least not as far as representative participation is concerned.

Yet, a closer look reveals that something *has* happened.

First of all, significant actors at the EU level, including the Commission, have consistently acted on the conviction that European economic integration cannot succeed without a certain harmonization of the 'superstructure' of economic activities. The Commission's most persistent argument for a common regulation of employee participation has been that companies as well as employees must have equal rights and obligations across the member states. Here, as on other questions, the Commission has maintained the necessity of 'spillover' changes in the industrial relations area in order to achieve the main objective of the Community, a genuine economic integration. Moreover, it is a fact that (a) the EU actually has already introduced common rules for participation in relation to mass redundancies, transfers of undertakings, health and safety, and information and consultation in multinational companies; and that (b) the proposals for a European Company Statute and a Fifth Directive are still on the EU agenda.

Secondly, it is important to note the convergence that has already taken place in the orientations and positions of European trade unions and employers' organizations. Interest articulation in relation to employee participation has moved from being essentially national in character to being European. In the 1970s the attitudes and reactions of trade unions and employers' associations were mainly based on widely diverging national experiences, and in this sense one may see the EC proposals of that time as premature. Today, both sides have developed common policies on employee participation, and have been through long and detailed discussions about the possible consequences of the EU proposals.

So, in spite of many years of seeming standstill, it can be concluded that a convergence actually has occurred, and that, given continued economic integration within the EU, this process will most likely continue in the future. It is not to be expected, however, that we will see a precise equalization between the EU member states as to the intensity and specific forms of participation. Indeed, the latest versions of the Commission's proposals on participation pay great attention to national diversities. Moreover, as argued in chapter 1, the development of a common ground for participation and its promotion to a central role in workplace industrial relations, is a complicated historical process. The behaviour of managers and employees cannot be changed overnight by a top–bottom approach; nor can deeply rooted and fundamentally diverse national industrial relations cultures, including traditional management and union strategies. For these reasons European participation structures will continue to be uneven to a considerable extent.

To speak of a European model for employee participation may still be premature. Yet, in particular, the adoption of the directive on European Works Councils signals that the principle of representative participation is going to remain an integral part of industrial relations within the European Union. A later British consent to this principle, and EU adoptions of the European Company Statute and the Fifth Directive, would strengthen this scenario considerably. It would add substance to the, as yet, essentially normative concept of a European model.

What will happen if the process of convergence does not continue as foreseen above? In my opinion, it would imply a weakening of the economic and social cohesion of the European Union. The Union would increasingly be divided between regions where capital invests in order to have a highly motivated, reliable, creative and participating workforce at its disposal, and regions where what matters is primarily the cheapness and obedience of labour. With a continuing internationalization of property relations, another likely consequence is the gradual erosion of employee participation rights based on national regulations. Within such a perspective, participation loses its character of compromise between class interests, and thereby a great deal of its 'Europeanness'. It is reduced essentially to a management tool.

A European model or not – that remains the question.

References

Albert M. (1993): *Capitalism against Capitalism*, London, Whurr Publishers.

Aldrich P.T. (1988): *Inddragelse af hensyn til arbejdsforholdene i den tekniske planlægning*, Lyngby, Institut for Arbejdsmiljø, Danmarks Tekniske Højskole.

Alhøj E. (1992): Medarbejderindflydelse stor succes, pp. 4–13 in *Det Fri Aktuelt* (tillæg), May 1.

Alonso Olea M. & Rodriguez-Sañudo F. (1988): Spain, in R. Blanpain (ed.), *International Encyclopedia for Labour Law and Industrial Relations*, Deventer, Kluwer.

Altmann N. (1992a): Unions' policies towards new technologies in the 1980s – an example from the metal industry, pp. 361–85 in N. Altmann, C. Köhler & P. Meil (eds), *Technology and Work in German Industry*, London, Routledge.

Altmann N. (1992b): Rationalization strategies and representation of worker interests, pp. 385–400 in N. Altmann, C. Köhler & P. Meil (eds), *Technology and Work in German Industry*, London, Routledge.

Altmann N., Köhler C. & Meil P. (eds) (1992): *Technology and Work in German Industry*, London, Routledge.

Andersen J.G. (1993): Politisk deltagelse i 1990 sammenlignet med 1979, pp. 45–75 in J. Andersen, A.-D. Christensen, K. Langberg, B. Siim & L. Torpe, *Medborgerskab: Demokrati og politisk deltagelse*, Herning, Systime.

Andersen O.S. (1991): *Samarbejde på dansk*, Copenhagen, DA/LO.

Arbejdsmiljøfondet (1980): *Bemærkninger til bekendtgørelse om virksomhedernes sikkerheds- og sundhedsarbejde*, Copenhagen, Arbejdsmiljøfondet.

Beirne M. & Ramsay H. (eds) (1992a): *Information Technology and Workplace Democracy*, London and New York, Routledge.

Beirne M. & Ramsay H. (1992b): A creative offensive? Participative design systems and the question of control, pp. 92–121 in M. Beirne & H. Ramsay (eds), *Information Technology and Workplace Democracy*, London and New York, Routledge.

Benedictus R., Bourn C. & Neal A.C. (eds) (1977): *Industrial Democracy: the Implications of the Bullock Report*, University of Leicester.

Betten L. (ed.) (1991): *The Future of European Social Policy*, Deventer/Boston, Kluwer.

Biagi M. (1990): Forms of employee participation at the workplace, pp. 197–239 in R. Blanpain (ed.), *Comparative Labour Law and Industrial Relations in Industrialised Market Economies*, vol. 1, Deventer, Kluwer.

Biagi M. (1993): Employee representation in small and medium-sized enterprises: a comparative overview, pp. 847–65 in International Industrial Relations Association, *Economic and Political Changes in Europe: Implications on Industrial Relations*, Bari, Cacucci Editore.

Blauner R. (1964): *Alienation and Freedom*, Chicago, Chicago University Press.

Blumberg P. (1968): *Industrial Democracy: the Sociology of Participation*, London, Constable.

Bolle de Bal M. (1989): Participation: its contradictions, paradoxes, and promises, pp. 11–26 in C.J. Lammers & G. Széll (eds), *International Handbook of Participation in Organizations, Vol. I: Organizational Democracy*, Oxford, Oxford University Press.

Braverman H. (1974): *Labour and Monopoly Capital: the Degradation of Work in the Twentieth Century*, New York, Monthly Review Press.

Brown R.K. (1992): *Understanding Industrial Organizations: Theoretical Perspectives in Industrial Sociology*, London and New York, Routledge.

Bullock A. (1977): *Report of the Committee of Inquiry on Industrial Democracy*, London, HMSO.

Burawoy M. (1985): *The Politics of Production: Factory Regimes under Capitalism and Socialism*, London, Verso.

Burg U., Fälling C. & Lollike L. (1982): *Lov om arbejdsmiljø – kommentarer og praksis*, Copenhagen, Arbejdsmiljøfondet.

Carley M. (1993): Voluntary initiatives – an update, *P + European Participation Monitor*, 6: 14–22.

Castillo J.J. (1992): *Nuevas Formas de Organización del Trabajo y Implicación directa en España*, Dublin, European Foundation.

CC.OO (1989): *Propuesta Sindical Prioritaria*, Madrid, CC.OO.

CEC (1972): Proposal for Fifth Directive . . . as regards the structure of Sociétés Anonymes and the powers and obligations of their organ, *Official Journal of the European Communities*, no. C 131, 13 December.

CEC (1974): Social action programme, *Bulletin of the European Communities*, Supplement 2/74.

CEC (1975a): Proposal for a council regulation on the statute for European companies, *Bulletin of the European Communities*, Supplement 4/75.

CEC (1975b): Employee participation and company structure, *Bulletin of the European Communities*, Supplement 8/75.

CEC (1975c): Multinational undertakings and community regulations, *Bulletin of the European Communities*, Supplement 8/75.

CEC (1975d): Directive 75/129/EEC on the approximation of the laws of the member states relating to collective redundancies, Brussels, CEC.

CEC (1977): Directive 77/187/EEC on the approximation of the laws of the member states relating to the safeguarding of employees' rights in the event of transfers of undertakings, businesses or parts of businesses, Brussels, CEC.

CEC (1980): Proposal for a Directive on procedures for informing and consulting the employees of undertakings with complex structures in particular transnational undertakings, *Official Journal of the European Communities*, no. C 297, 15 November.

CEC (1983a): Amended proposal for a Council Directive on procedures for informing and consulting employees of undertakings with complex structures, in particular transnational undertakings, *Official Journal of the European Communities*, 12 August.

CEC (1983b): Amended proposal for a Fifth Directive . . . concerning the structure of public limited companies and the powers and obligations of their organs, *Official Journal of the European Communities*, no. C 240/2, 9 September.

CEC (1985): White Paper on completing the internal market (COM(85) 310 final), Brussels.

CEC (1988): Memorandum on the Statute for a European Company (COM(88) 320 final), *Bulletin of the European Communities*, Supplement 3/88, Brussels.

CEC (1989a): Proposal for a Council regulation on the Statute for a European Company (COM (89) 268 final – SYN 218), Brussels, CEC.

CEC (1989b): Proposal for a Council Directive complementing the Statute for a European Company with regard to the involvement of employees in the European Company (COM (89) 268 final – SYN 219), Brussels, CEC.

CEC (1989c): Council Directive on the introduction of measures to encourage improvements in the safety and health of workers at work (89/391/EEC), June 12, Brussels, CEC.

CEC (1990a): Community Charter of the Fundamental Social Rights of Workers, pp. 46–50 in *Social Europe* 1/90, Brussels.

CEC (1990b): Action programme relating to the implementation of the Community Charter of Basic Social Rights for Workers (COM (89) 568 final), pp. 51–76 in *Social Europe* 1/90, Brussels.

CEC (1990c): Proposal for a Council Directive on the establishment of a European Works Council in Community-scale undertakings or groups of undertakings for the purposes of informing and consulting employees (COM(90) 581 final), Brussels, CEC.

CEC (1991): Amended proposal for a Council Directive on the establishment of a European Works Council in Community-scale undertakings or groups of undertakings for the purposes of informing and consulting employees (COM(91) 345 final), Brussels, CEC.

CEC (1992): Council Directive 92/56/EEC amending Directive 75/129/EEC on the approximation of the laws of the Member States relating to collective redundancies, *Official Journal of the European Communities*, no. L 245/3, 26 August.

CEC (1994): Proposed Council Directive on the establishment of European committees or procedures in Community-scale undertakings and Community-scale groups of undertakings for the purposes of informing and consulting employees, *Official Journal of the European Communities*, no. 135/94, April.

Christensen A. (1979): *Arbejdsorganisation og konjunkturudvikling*, Aalborg, Aalborg Universitetsforlag.

Christensen P.M., Gammelgaard B., Hansen K., Knudsen H., Mogensen H. & Valeur C. (1974): *Tillidsmandsrapporten*, Århus, Modtryk.

Clausen C. & Lorentzen B. (1993): Workplace implications of FMS and CIM in Denmark and Sweden, *New Technology, Work and Employment*, 8, 1, 21–31.

Clausen C., Lorentzen B. & Rasmussen L.B. (eds) (1992): *Deltagelse i teknologisk udvikling. Eksempler på forskning og udvikling i samarbejde med arbejdspladser, organisationer og lokalsamfund*, Copenhagen, Fremad.

Clegg H.A. (1976): *The System of Industrial Relations in Great Britain*, Oxford, Blackwell.

Coates D. (1975): *The Labour Party and the Struggle for Socialism*, Cambridge, Cambridge University Press.

Coates K. & Topham T. (1970): *Workers' Control*, London, Panther.

Council Resolution Concerning a Social Action Programme of 21 January (1974), pp. 74–9 in A.C. Neal & F.B. Wright (eds), *The European Communities' Health and Safety Legislation*, London, Chapman & Hall, 1992.

Cressey P. (1992): Trade unions and new technology: European experience and strategic questions, pp. 236–65 in M. Beirne & H. Ramsay (eds), *Information Technology and Workplace Democracy*, London and New York, Routledge.

Crouch C. (1990): United Kingdom: the rejection of compromise, pp. 326–55 in G. Baglioni & C. Crouch (eds), *European Industrial Relations: the Challenge of Flexibility*, London, Sage.

Crouch C. (1993): *Industrial Relations and European State Traditions*, Oxford, Clarendon Press.

Dale E. (1954): Union–management cooperation, pp. 359–73 in A. Kornhauser, R. Dubin & A.M. Ross (eds), *Industrial Conflict*, New York, McGraw-Hill.

Daniel W.W. (1987): *Workplace Industrial Relations and Technical Change*, London, Frances Pinter/Policy Studies Institute.

Daniel W.W. & Millward N. (1984): *Workplace Industrial Relations in Britain: The DE/PSI/ESRC Survey*, London, Heinemann.

Dansk Magisterforening (1991): *Faglig håndbog*, Copenhagen, Dansk Magisterforening.

Deery S. (1989): Determinants of trade union influence over technological change, *New Technology, Work and Employment*, 4, 2: 117–30.

Deery S. (1992): Trade union involvement and influence over technological decisions, pp. 212–36 in M. Beirne & H. Ramsay (eds), *Information Technology and Workplace Democracy*, London and New York, Routledge.

Dowdy T. (1990): The emergence of the social dimension of the European Economic Community, *Brigham Young University Law Review*, 4: 1667–86.

Due J., Madsen J.S. & Jensen C.S. (1993): *Den danske model: en historisk sociologisk analyse af det danske aftalesystem*, Copenhagen, Jurist- og Økonomforbundets Forlag.

Durán López F., Montoya Melgar A. & Sala Franco T. (1987): *El ordenamiento laboral español y los limites a la autonomia de las partes y a las facultades del empresario*, Madrid, Ministerio de Trabajo y Seguridad.

Economic and Social Committee of the EC (1991): Opinion on the proposal for a Council Directive on the establishment of a European Works Council in Community-scale undertakings or groups of undertakings for the purposes of informing and consulting employees, *Official Journal of the European Communities*, no. C 39, 2 February.

Edmonds J. (1977): The Bullock Committee's Report and collective bargaining, in R. Benedictus, C. Brown & A.C. Neal (eds), *Industrial Democracy: the Implications of the Bullock Report*, University of Leicester.

Edwards R. (1979): *Contested Terrain: the Transformation of the Workplace in the Twentieth Century*, New York, Basic Books.

EIRR (1990): Employee participation in Europe. Works councils, worker directors and other forms of participation in 15 European countries, *European Industrial Relations Review Report*, no. 4, London.

EIRR (1994a) *European Industrial Relations Review*, 247, August.

EIRR (1994b) *European Industrial Relations Review*, 248, September.

Elam M.J. (1990): Puzzling out the post-Fordist debate: technology, markets and institutions, *Economic and Industrial Democracy*, 11, 1: 9–39.

Employment Observatory (1992) *Trends*, no. 8, Brussels, SYSDEM/CEC.

Employment Observatory (1993) *Policies*, no. 41, Brussels, MISEP/CEC.

Endruweit G. & Berger G. (1986): The functioning of institutionalised forms of workers' participation – seen from a social science perspective, pp. 123–47 in International Industrial Relations Association, *Institutional Forms of Workers' Participation, with Special Reference to the Federal Republic of Germany*, Geneva, IIRA, ILO.

ET (1989) Estatuto de Trabajadores, printed in M. Rodriguez-Piñero & A.O. Aviles, *Legislación laboral*, Madrid, Tecnos.

ETUC (1989): *Resolution on the Proposal for a Council Regulation on the Statute for the European Company and for a Council Directive with regard to the involvement of employees in the European Company*, 26 September, Brussels, ETUC.

ETUI (1990): *Workers' Representation and Rights in the Workplace in Western Europe*, Brussels, ETUI.

European Foundation for the Improvement of Living and Working Conditions (1990): *Roads to Participation in Technological Change – Attitudes and Experiences*, Luxembourg, CEC.

Evans S. (1991): Industrial relations in Britain after Thatcher, pp. 97–120 in H.J. Jeppesen & J. Lind (eds), *Changes in Labour Market and Industrial Relations in Europe*, Yearbook 1991, Centre for Labour Market Research, University of Aalborg.

168   *Employee participation in Europe*

Federal Minister of Labour and Social Affairs (1980): *Co-determination in the Federal Republic of Germany*, Bonn.
Fox A. (1974): *Beyond Contract: Work, Power and Trust Relations*, London, Faber & Faber.
Friedman A.L. (1977): *Industry and Labour: Class Struggle at Work and Monopoly Capitalism*, London, Macmillan.
Fröhlich D., Fuchs D. & Krieger H. (1989): *New Information Technology and Participation in Europe – the Potential for Social Dialogue*, Luxembourg, EF/CEC.
Fröhlich D., Gill C. & Krieger H. (1991): *Roads to Participation in the European Community: Increasing Prospects of Employee Representatives in Technological Change*, Dublin/Luxembourg, EF.
Fürstenberg F. (1978): *Workers' Participation in Management in the Federal Republic of Germany*, Geneva, ILO.
Gallie D. (1978): *In Search of the New Working Class: Automation and Social Integration within the Capitalist Enterprise*, Cambridge, Cambridge University Press.
García Murcia J. (1986): La participación sindical en la empresa pública: el acuerdo de 16 de enero de 1986, *Claridad*, 13: 25–39.
García Murcia J. (1990): Concertación y participación sindical en la empresa pública, pp. 253–60 in A. Ojeda Avilés (ed.), *La concertación social tras la crisis*, Barcelona, Editorial Ariel.
George S. (1991): *Politics and Polity in the European Community*, Oxford, Oxford University Press.
Gevers J.K.M. (1983): Workers' participation in management in health and safety in the EEC: the role of representative institutions, *International Labour Review*, 122, 4: 411–29.
Gill C. (1985): *Work, Unemployment and the New Technology*, Cambridge, Polity Press.
Gill C. (1991): British trade unionism in retreat in the 1980s, pp. 193–214 in H.J. Jeppesen & J. Lind (eds), *Changes in Labour Market and Industrial Relations in Europe*, Yearbook 1991, Centre for Labour Market Research, University of Aalborg.
Gill C. (1993): Participation in health and safety within the European Community, Research Paper no. 14/93, Management Studies, Cambridge University.
Gill C. & Krieger H. (1992): Participation in work organization: recent results from a European Community survey, Research Paper no. 23/92, Management Studies, Cambridge University.
Gjerding A.N., Johnson B., Kallehauge L., Lundvall B.Å. & Madsen P.T. (1990): *Den forsvundne produktivitet: industriel udvikling i firsernes Danmark*, Copenhagen, Jurist- og Økonomforbundets Forlag.
Glendon A.I. & Booth R.T. (1982): Worker participation in occupational health and safety in Britain, *International Labour Review*, 121, 4: 399–416.
Gold M. & Hall M. (1990): *Legal Regulation and the Practice of Employee Participation in the European Community*, Working Paper no. EF/WP/90/40/EN, Dublin, EF.
Gold M. & Hall M. (1992): *Report on European Information and Consultation in Multinational Companies – an Evaluation of Practice*, Dublin/Luxembourg, EF.
Gold M. & Hall M. (1993): Experience with voluntary initiatives, *P+ European Participation Monitor*, 6: 9–14.
Gouldner A.W. (1980): *The Two Marxisms: Contradictions and Anomalies in the Development of Theory*, New York, Seabury Press.
Grab C. & Krüger K. (1993): Las negociaciones colectivas y las aplicaciones de tecnologias en empresas: los derechos de participación – marco legal y realización, mimeo, Barcelona 1993.

Haire M. (1954): Group dynamics in the industrial situation, pp. 373–86 in A. Kornhauser, R. Dubin & A.M. Ross (eds), *Industrial Conflict*, New York, McGraw-Hill.

Hall M. (1992): Legislating for employee participation: a case study of the European Works Council directive, *Warwick Papers in Industrial Relations*, no. 39.

Hall M., Marginson P. & Sisson K. (1993): Researching the European Works Council, *P + European Participation Monitor*, 6: 32–6.

Hansen K. (1991): *Europeiske selskap – medbestemmelse og bedriftsdemokrati*, Oslo, FAFO.

Hill S. (1981): *Competition and Control at Work*, Cambridge, Mass., MIT Press.

Hussey R. & Marsh A. (1983): *Disclosure of Information and Employee Reporting*, Aldershot, Gower.

Hyman R. (1975): *Industrial Relations: a Marxist Introduction*, London, Macmillan.

Hyman R. (1990): Plus ça change? The theory of production and the production of theory, pp. 89–110 in L. Dalsgaard, H. Knudsen & P. Rasmussen (eds), *Årbog for Arbejdsmarkedsforskning 1990, Tema: Fleksibilitet*, Centre for Labour Market Research, University of Aalborg.

Hyman R. & Fryer B. (1975): Trade unions – sociology and political economy, pp. 150–214 in J.B. McKinlay (ed.), *Processing People: Cases in Organizational Behaviour*, London, Holt, Rinehart & Winston.

Hyman R. & Streeck W. (eds) (1988): *New Technology and Industrial Relations*, Oxford, Oxford University Press.

IDE International Research Group (1981): Industrial democracy in Europe: differences and similarities across countries and hierarchies, *Organization Studies*, 2, 2: 113–30.

ILO (1985): *The Trade Union Situation and Industrial Relations in Spain*, Geneva, ILO.

IP Dansk Institut for Personalerådgivning, Price Waterhouse & Handelshøjskolen i København/IKO (1991): *HRM 91: Human Resource Management i danske virksomheder*, Copenhagen.

Jacobi O. & Müller-Jentsch W. (1990): West Germany: continuity and structural change, pp. 127–54 in G. Baglioni & C. Crouch (eds), *European Industrial Relations: the Challenge of Flexibility*, London, Sage.

Jakobsen D. & Clausen C. (1991): *Tør Danmark også? Programmer for udvikling af de menneskelige ressourcer i arbejdslivet*, Copenhagen, LO.

Jensen C.S., Madsen J.S. & Due J. (1993): Towards a European IR-system? The implications of the Maastricht Treaty for Danish industrial relations, mimeo, Department of Sociology, University of Copenhagen.

Jones B. (1989): When certainty fails: inside the factory of the future, pp. 44–59 in S. Woods (ed.), *The Transformation of Work? Skill, Deskilling and the Labour Process*, London, Hutchinson.

Kaiero A. (1988): Participación de los trabajadores en la empresa. Relaciones laborales y contexto social en Europa y en España, *Estudios de Deusto*, 36: 391–435, Bilbao.

Kern H. & Schumann M. (1985): *Das Ende der Arbeitsteilung? Rationalisierung in der industriellen Produktion*, Munich, C.H. Beck Verlag.

Kerr C. (1983): *The Future of Industrial Societies: Convergence or Continuing Diversity*, Cambridge, Mass./London, Harvard University Press.

Kerr C., Dunlop J.T., Harbison F. & Myers C.A. (1962): *Industrialism and Industrial Man: the Problems of Labor and Management in Economic Growth*, London, Heinemann.

Kiil O. & Heide J. (1986): *Arbejdsmiljø og teknisk planlægning*, Copenhagen, Arbejdsmiljøfondet.

Kissler L. (1989): Co-determination research in the Federal Republic of Germany: a review, pp. 74–91 in C.J. Lammers & G. Széll (eds), *International Handbook of Participation in Organizations, Vol. I: Organizational Democracy*, Oxford, Oxford University Press.

Knudsen H. (1983): *Disciplinering til lønarbejde*, Aalborg, Aalborg Universitetsforlag.

Knudsen H. (1991): Industrial relations in Spain: continuity and change, pp. 79–96 in H.J. Jeppesen & J. Lind (eds), *Changes in Labour Market and Industrial Relations in Europe*, Centre for Labour Market Research, University of Aalborg.

Knudsen H. & Sandahl J. (1974): *Arbejdskamp i Storbritanien. Strejker og fabriksbesættelser i begyndelsen af 1970'erne*, Århus, Modtryk.

Kocik A. & Grünbaum H. (1948): Organisationens historie, pp. 99–226 in De samvirkende Fagforbund, *Under Samvirkets Flag*, Copenhagen, De samvirkende Fagforbund.

Kofoed L.B. (ed.) (1990): *Planlægning af et godt arbejdsmiljø*, Institut for Samfundsudvikling og Planlægning, Aalborg Universitetscenter.

Kolvenbach W. & Hanau P. (1987/94): *Handbook on European Employee Co-Management*, Deventer, Kluwer.

Labour Party (1986): Statement to Conference, *People at Work: New Rights, New Responsibilities*, London, the Labour Party.

Lammers C.J. & Széll G. (1989): Concluding reflections, pp. 315–30 in C.J. Lammers & G. Széll (eds), *International Handbook of Participation in Organizations, Vol. I: Organizational Democracy*, Oxford, Oxford University Press.

Lane C. (1989): *Management and Labour in Europe*, Aldershot, Edward Elgar.

Langergaard I. (1991): Virksomheder blæser på sikkerheden, in *Det fri Aktuelt*, 16 August.

Lapeyre J. (1990): In search of the lost social dimension, pp. 25–8 in *Social Europe* 1/90, Brussels.

Lecher W. (ed.) (1994): *Trade Unions in the European Union*, London, Lawrence & Wishart.

Leminsky G. (1986): Institutional forms of workers' participation, with special reference to the Federal Republic of Germany – seen from a union's point of view, pp. 147–61 in International Industrial Relations Association, *Institutionalised Forms of Workers' Participation, with Special Reference to the Federal Republic of Germany*, Geneva, IIRA/ILO.

Levinson C. (1972): *International Trade Unionism*, London, Allen & Unwin.

Ley 2/(1991) sobre derechos de información de los representantes de los trabajadores en materia de contratación, 7 January, Madrid.

Lind J. (1991): Industrial relations and labour market regulations in Denmark, pp. 37–54 in H.J. Jeppesen & J. Lind (eds), *Changes in Labour Market and Industrial Relations in Europe*, Centre for Labour Market Research, University of Aalborg.

Littler C.R. (1982): *The Development of the Labour Process in Capitalist Societies*, London, Heinemann.

LO (1991a): *Det udviklende arbejde*, Copenhagen, LO.

LO (1991b): *Fremtidens arbejdsret*, Copenhagen, LO.

LO handlingsplan (1991): in *LO-Bladet*, no. 33, 21 November.

Lockwood D. (1958): *The Blackcoated Worker*, London, Allen & Unwin.

Lorentzen B. (1990): Arbejderdeltagelse i teknologiplanlægning: rationaliseringsmiddel eller interessevaretagelse?, *På tværs*, 3: 14–32, Lyngby, Danmarks Tekniske Højskole.

Lov om universiteter m.fl. (1992), 23 December, Copenhagen.

Lucas Marín A. (1990): La democracia industrial: el autogobierno en las organizaciones economicas, *Revista de Trabajo*, 97: 141–53.

Lund R. (1991): Evolution of co-operation systems in Denmark, pp. 177–93 in H.J. Jeppesen & J. Lind (eds), *Changes in Labour Market and Industrial Relations in Europe*, Centre for Labour Market Research, University of Aalborg.

Macpherson C.B. (1962): *The Political Theory of Possessive Individualism*, Oxford, Oxford University Press.

Mallet S. (1975): *The New Working Class*, Nottingham, Spokesman.

Martens H. (1992): Weniger für die als mit der Belegschaft, *Die Mitbestimmung*, 11: 36–9.

Martín Valverde A. (1991): *European Employment and Industrial Relations Glossary: Spain*, London, EF/Sweet & Maxwell.

Martín Valverde A., Rodriguez-Sañudo F. & García Murcia J. (1991): *Derecho del Trabajo*, Madrid, Tecnos.

Marx K. (1973): *Das Kapital. Kritik der politischen Ökonomie*, Berlin, Dietz Verlag.

Maurice M., Sellier F. & Silvestre J.J. (1986): *The Social Foundations of Industrial Power: a Comparison of France and Germany*, Cambridge Mass., MIT Press.

Merrifierd L.S. (1982): La participación del trabajador en las decisiones de las empresas, *Revista Española de Derecho del Trabajo*, 12: 501–20.

Methven J. (1977): Debate on industrial democracy: the CBI view, *Socialist Commentary*, March, 9–10.

Miguélez F. (1993): The impact of multinational companies in the modern way of human resource management in Spain. Paper presented to the Conference on Multinationals and Human Resource Management, Barcelona, 19–21 November.

Millward N. & Stevens M. (1986): *British Workplace Industrial Relations 1980–84: the DE/ESRC/PSI/ACAS Surveys*, Aldershot, Gower.

Millward N., Stevens M., Smart D. & Hawes W.R. (1992): First findings from the 1990 Workplace Industrial Relations Survey, mimeo.

MISEP (Mutual Information System on Employment Policies) (1992): *Denmark – Institutions, Procedures and Measures*, Institute for Policy Research, Leiden, MISEP/CEC.

Møller N., Langaa Jensen P. & Broberg Jensen O. (1988): *Arbejdsmåder i sikkerheds-gruppen*, Copenhagen, Arbejdsmiljøfondet.

Monero Pérez J.L. & Moreno Vida M.N. (1987): Cambio tecnológico, cualificación y formación profesional, pp. 269–313 in F. Rodriguez-Sañudo & A. Martín Valverde (eds), *Contrato de trabajo y formación profesional. Consecuencias laborales y sociales de la integración de España en la Communidad Europea*, Madrid, Ministerio de Trabajo y Seguridad Social.

Morris T. & Wood S. (1991): Testing the survey method: continuity and change in British industrial relations, *Work, Employment and Society*, 5, 2: 259–82.

Müller J. (1991): Towards a conceptual framework for social planning of technology. Paper presented to the Colloquium on Social Mastery of Technology, Lyon, September.

Müller-Jentsch W. (1986): *Soziologie der industriellen Beziehungen*, Frankfurt am Main, Campus.

Müller-Jentsch W., Rehermann K. & Sperling H.J. (1992): Socio-technical rationalisation and negotiated work organization: recent trends in Germany, pp. 93–112 in OECD, *New Directions in Work Organization: the Industrial Relations Response*, Paris, OECD.

Müller-Jentsch W. & Sperling H.J. (1992): New technology and employee involvement in banking, mimeo.

Munch P. (1993): Ny strid om koncernsamarbejde, in *LO-Bladet*, no. 20, 26 October.

Neal A.C. & Wright F.B. (eds) (1992): *The European Communities' Health and Safety Legislation*, London, Chapman & Hall.

Neergaard P. (1990): Teknologiaftaler: aftaler og love af betydning for indførelse af ny teknologi, *Økonomistyring og Informatik*, 6, 3: 143–66.

Nichols T. & Armstrong P. (1976): *Workers Divided: a Study in Shop Floor Politics*, Glasgow, Fontana/Collins.

Nielsen R. (1987): *Lærebog i arbejdsret*, Copenhagen, Jurist- og Økonomforbundets Forlag.

Pelling H. (1971): *A History of British Trade Unionism*, Harmondsworth, Penguin.

Pérez Pérez M. (1987): Formación profesional y nuevos sistemas tecnológicos, pp. 313–37 in F. Rodriguez-Sañudo & A. Martín Valverde (eds), *Contrato de trabajo y formación profesional: consecuencias laborales y sociales de la integración de España en la Communidad Europea*, Madrid, Ministerio de Trabajo y Seguridad Social.

Pignon D. & Querzola J.V. (1976): Dictatorship and democracy in production, pp. 63–100 in A. Gorz (ed.), *The Division of Labour: the Labour Process and Class Struggle in Modern Capitalism*, Hassocks, Brighton, Harvester Press.

Piore M. & Sabel C. (1984): *The Second Industrial Divide*, New York, Basic Books.

Poole M. (1978): *Workers' Participation in Industry*, London, Routledge & Kegan Paul.

Poole M. (1986a): *Towards a New Industrial Democracy: Workers' Participation in Industry*, London, Routledge & Kegan Paul.

Poole M. (1986b): *Industrial Relations: Origins and Patterns of National Diversity*, London, Routledge & Kegan Paul.

Price R. (1988): Information, consultation and the control of new technology, pp. 249–62 in R. Hyman & W. Streeck (eds), *New Technology and Industrial Relations*, Oxford, Oxford University Press.

Ramsay H. (1983): Evolution or cycle? Worker participation in the 1970s and 1980s, pp. 203–26 in C. Crouch & F. Heller (eds), *Organizational Democracy and Political Processes*, London, John Wiley & Sons.

Regini M. (1992): Human resource management and industrial relations in European companies, pp. 121–31 in International Industrial Relations Association, *Human Resource Management: Implications for Teaching, Theory, Research and Practice in Industrial Relations*, Sydney, IIRA.

Rivero Lamas J. (1986): *Limitación de los poderes empresariales y democracia industrial*, Zaragoza, Universidad de Zaragoza.

Rivero Lamas J. & García Blasco J. (1987): Los derechos de información en la empresa en el marco europeo e internacional y en España, pp. 493–534 in F. Rodriguez-Sañudo & A. Martín Valverde (eds), *Contrato de trabajo y formación profesional: consecuencias laborales y sociales de la integración de España en la Communidad Europea*, Madrid, Ministerio de Trabajo y Seguridad Social.

Rodriguez-Piñero M. & Ojeda Avilés A. (1989): *Legislación laboral*, Madrid, Tecnos.

Rodriguez-Sañudo F. (1979): La participación de los trabajadores en la empresa, *Revista de Política Social*, 121: 415–37.

Rodriguez-Sañudo F. (1988): Jurisprudencia reciente sobre la actividad del comité de empresa, *Revista Española de Derecho del Trabajo*, 36: 621–33.

Rojot J. (1986): Employers' response to technological change, pp. 183–201 in International Industrial Relations Association, *Technological Change and Labour Relations*, Geneva, IIRA/ILO.

Samarbejdsnævnet (1991): *De gode eksemplers klub*, Copenhagen, DA/LO.

Saracibar A. (1986): El reto sindical de la participación obrera en España, *Claridad*, 13: 5–25.

Schmidt E. (1971): *Die verhinderte Neuordnung*, Frankfurt am Main, Europäische Verlagsanstalt.

Schmitthoff C.M. (1977): The Bullock Committee and the EEC, pp. 6.1–6.12 in R. Benedictus, C. Brown & A.C. Neal (eds), *Industrial Democracy: the Implications of the Bullock Report*, University of Leicester.

Schneider W. (1989): Betriebsverfassungsrecht, pp. 391–402 in M. Kittner (ed.), *Gewerkschaftsjahrbuch 1989*, Cologne.

Schregle J. (1978): Co-determination in the Federal Republic of Germany: a comparative view, *International Labour Review*, 117, 1: 81–99.

Schregle J. (1986): The German model of institutionalised workers' participation in the international context of workers' participation, pp. 171–83 in International Industrial Relations Association, *Institutionalised Forms of Workers' Participation, with Special Reference to the Federal Republic of Germany*, Geneva, IIRA/ILO.

Scott A. (1991): Consultation and communication, *Employment Gazette*, 99, 9: 507–12.

Senovilla H.M. & de la Torre M.D.R. (1987): Los convenios de junio, julio, agosto y septiembre: la participación de los trabajadores en la empresa. Funciones de los representantes unitarios, *Relaciones Laborales*, 24: 111–36.

Simonsen, B. (1991): *Nordiskt koncernfackligt samarbete: en argumentationsanalys*, Göteborg, NordFram.

Sobrera M.A.C. (1985): Protectión penal de la participación de los trabajadores en la empresa, pp. 131–43 in *Jornados organizadas por jueces para la democracia*, Santiago de Compostela.

Sperling H.J. (1991): Arbeitsmarkt und industrielle Beziehungen in der Bundesrepublik Deutschland in den achtziger Jahren, pp. 55–79 in H.J. Jeppesen & J. Lind (eds), *Changes in Labour Market and Industrial Relations in Europe*, Centre for Labour Market Research, University of Aalborg.

Springer B. (1992): *The Social Dimension of 1992: Europe Faces a New EC*, New York, Praeger.

Storey J & Sisson K. (1993): *Managing Human Resources and Industrial Relations*, Buckingham, Open University Press.

Streeck W. (1984): *Industrial Relations in West Germany: a Case Study of the Car Industry*, London, Heinemann.

Svane V. (1965): Tillidsmandssystemet, pp. 98–120 in V. Nielsen & V. Svane (eds), *Arbejdsforhold historisk og aktuelt*, Copenhagen, AOF.

Sveistrup P.P. (1926): *Bedriftsraad*, Copenhagen, Folkeuniversitetsudvalget.

Taylor R. (1977): Debate on industrial democracy: the trade unions and Bullock, in *Socialist Commentary*, 5–7 March.

Teague P. & Grahl J. (1992): *Industrial Relations and European Integration*, London, Lawrence & Wishart.

Thompson E.P. (1978): *The Poverty of Theory & Other Essays*, London, Merlin.

Thüssing R. (1986): The functioning of institutionalised forms of workers' participation: seen from an employers' association's point of view, pp. 161–71 in International Industrial Relations Association, *Institutionalised Forms of Workers' Participation, with Special Reference to the Federal Republic of Germany*, Geneva, IIRA/ILO.

TUC (1988): *Maximising the Benefits, Minimising the Costs: Report on Europe 1991*, London, TUC.

Tyszkiewicz Z.J.A. (1990): Employers' views on the Community Charter of Basic Social Rights for Workers, pp. 22–4 in *Social Europe* 1/90, Brussels.

UNICE (1989): *Summary of the UNICE position on the European Company Statute*, 25 October, Brussels, UNICE.

UNICE (1991): *Position Paper on the proposal for a European Works Councils Directive*, 4 March, Brussels, UNICE.

Vaca E.R. (1990): Los despidos colectivos por motivos económicos en la nueva legislación francesa, *Actualidad Laboral*, 42: 521–6.

Venturini P. (1988): *The European Social Dimension*, Brussels/Luxembourg, CEC.

de la Villa L.E. (1980): *La participación de los trabajadores en la empresa*, Madrid, Instituto de Estudios Económicos.

Visser J.V. (1993): Employee representation in West European workplaces, pp. 793–823 in International Industrial Relations Association, *Economic and Political Changes in Europe: Implications on Industrial Relations*, Bari, Cacucci Editore.

Vogel L. (1991): *A Survey of Occupational Health and Safety Services in the Member States of the European Communities and the European Free Trade Association*, Brussels, ETUC.

Vogel L. (1992): *Evolution of Preventive Services in the Workplace and the Implementation of the Community's Framework Directive 89/391: Comparative Study in the EEC and EFTA Countries*, Brussels, ETUC.

Vroom V.H. & Jago A.G. (1988): *The New Leadership: Managing Participation in Organizations*, Englewood Cliffs, NJ, Prentice Hall.

Walker C.R. (1954): Work methods, working conditions, and morale, pp 345–59 in A. Kornhauser, R. Dubin & A.M. Ross (eds), *Industrial Conflict*, New York, McGraw-Hill.

Wedderburn, Lord (1977): Industrial democracy and company law, in R. Benedictus, C. Brown & A.C. Neal (eds), *Industrial Democracy: the Implications of the Bullock Report*, University of Leicester.

Wedderburn, Lord (1991): *Employment Rights in Britain and Europe: Selected Papers in Labour Law*, London, Lawrence & Wishart.

Weiss M. (1986): Institutionelle Formen der Mitwirkung von Arbeitnehmern mit Schwerpunkt Bundesrepublik Deutschland, pp. 53–71 in International Industrial Relations Association, *Institutionalised Forms of Workers' Participation, with Special Reference to the Federal Republic of Germany*, Geneva, IIRA/ILO.

Weiss M. (1987): *Labour Law and Industrial Relations in the Federal Republic of Germany*, Deventer, Kluwer.

Weiss M. (1989): Structural change and industrial relations in the Federal Republic of Germany, pp. 127–37 in International Industrial Relations Association, *Structural Change and Industrial Relations Strategies*, Geneva, IIRA/ILO.

Wood S. (ed.) (1989): *The Transformation of Work? Skill, Deskilling and the Labour Process*, London, Hutchinson.

Zoll R. (1991): Zur Notwendigkeit eines Neuansatzes gewerkschaftlicher Betriebspolitik in der Bundesrepublik, pp. 215–27 in H.J. Jeppesen & J. Lind (eds), *Changes in Labour Market and Industrial Relations in Europe*, Centre for Labour Market Research, University of Aalborg.

Index